fat
free
forever

Dianne Barker is a body-shaping expert,
fitness leader, personal trainer and a former
model. Dianne used the Body Shaping
System to recover her shape after giving
birth to her twin sons.

The cover of this book is a photograph
of Dianne taken after she successfully lost
40 kilos, following the Fat Free Forever
Body Shaping System!

Dianne with her twin sons Bentley and Beau.

fat
free
forever

The Body Shaping System

Dianne Barker

A Mandarin book
published by
Random House Australia Pty Ltd
20 Alfred Street, Milsons Point, NSW 2061
http://www.randomhouse.com.au

Typeset in Sabon by Asset Typesetting Pty Ltd
Printed and bound in Australia by Australian Book Connection
Front cover photo credits:
Hair: Baci Hair Design
Swimwear: Sue Rice Swimwear
Technical direction: Geoff Barker

National Library of Australia
  cataloguing-in-publication data:
    Barker, Dianne. Fat free forever: the body shaping system
ISBN 1 86330 526 2
    Reducing diets. I. Title
    613.25

The author and the publisher of this book are not medically trained and are not licensed to give medical advice. Always consult your doctor before embarking on any weight loss course. The facts provided are based on extensive research up until the publishing date, however the contents of products mentioned are subject to change by manufacturers from time to time and those contents may vary from those listed in this book.
  Although a useful guide when shopping, information in this book is not an endorsement or recommendation of any product, manufacturers, companies or individuals. The author and publisher disclaim any liability, damage or loss whatsoever arising directly or indirectly from the information contained in *Fat Free Forever*.

10 9 8 7 6

Contents

Section 3
How and Why

List of No-Fat Recipes

Section

1

What and Why

My Story

Life is full of choices.

If you eat fat, *you will* get fat.

If you overload on starchy carbohydrates (cereal, bread, potato, rice and pasta), *you will* get fat.

And if you starve yourself to be thin, *you will* get even fatter (eventually).

I have done the lot, and believe me – **it's true.**

•

From my mid-teens to early twenties, I went through the whole yoyo dieting thing, along with most of the other girls I knew. I would starve myself for a week just to fit into a pair of tiny jeans. I also suffered greatly when I had to eat in front of people. I was so nervous. One summer when I was away on holidays, I grazed on carrots and apples and drank only water for days on end. I certainly was the skinniest girl on the beach that summer!

> The greatest problem with not eating was
> that all I was doing was starving my muscle tissue
> and ruining my body shape.

Sure, I lost weight, but the less I ate, the more my poor body cried 'starvation', and clicked itself into a mode that was designed to store fat in times of 'famine' for protection. This made it nearly impossible to keep the fat off.

I learned that people are either emotional eaters or emotional starvers – I was both, depending on the circumstances!

> Did you know that your body sometimes feels falsely
> comforted when it absorbs the fat you eat?

This is a nutritional fact I'll discuss later. It's why emotional eaters usually head for the potato chips, buttered toast, peanut butter, hamburgers and chocolate. It takes a while to realise that comfort cannot come from a crinkle-cut anything.

During all of this unintended craziness, I didn't know about, or give a second thought to, what this was doing to my body's metabolism.

When I was growing up, we always had skim milk and lots of fresh fruit in our house. We would arrive home each afternoon after school and Mum would hand my sister and me a carrot on our way through the front door. Lemonade was a special treat, as were chocolate biscuits.

It wasn't that Mum had us on a diet, it was because she was conscious of healthy eating, and it just grew on us.

I knew there was something important missing in all this healthy eating though, and that was the knowledge of how to put it all together. What we didn't know then but we do now is that eating 'healthily' isn't necessarily going to give you the body shape of your dreams. A lot of health food is loaded with fats, and often the product – fish, for example – is great to start with, but when it's fried and accompanied by chips, it's lethal!

I actually thought (along with thousands of other teenagers), that the only way to lose weight quickly was to just stop eating. My poor Mum. Can you imagine? What hope did she have trying to convince her teenage daughter *(who knew everything)*, not to do this to her body! But now I realise, with hindsight, that I had so many excellent alternatives.

1987 was a heavy year for this teenage girl. My father suffered terribly from heart problems – he had unstable angina and a 90% closure of his left ventricle. This was caused by heredity, smoking for more than 30 years, and long-term bad eating habits. My Grandma was a single mum of eleven kids during the Depression, as my Grandpa died when Dad was just ten years old. This meant Grandma had to live on what you could call a tight budget. Fat came cheap!

It was hard for Dad to change his childhood eating habits. Even though Mum would prepare semi-healthy food, there would always be room for a few slices of bread and butter as well. Dad's weaknesses were choco-late and starchy carbs. And if we had a baked dinner (like so many other families in Australia), it would be dripping in dripping.

What happened to Dad shocked us all. It transformed our entire family's lifestyle for the better. My father survived major open-heart surgery and is alive and well today, more than ten years down the track.

> Sitting by his bedside taught me something worthwhile: we can change our lives and the quality of them by making certain choices.

Mum spent hours, days and weeks, seeking out and modifying all kinds of new recipes. She even turned the Heart Foundation and Pritikin diet books upside-down – taking out the tablespoon of oil here and teaspoon of margarine there. Nothing was going to get in the way of reducing Dad's cholesterol and weight. And, although she isn't a doctor, dietitian or even a personal trainer, she's smart and determined, and she did it!

Mum achieved unbelievable results from using no fat. Not only did my father's cholesterol shrink to a very low level, but his body shape changed dramatically, and he had the energy and enthusiasm of a man at least ten years his junior. Dad's doctor, Sydney heart surgeon Dr David Baron, was astounded at the short amount of time it took Mum to get Dad's cholesterol and weight down *before* his urgent heart operation.

Notice how I say Mum did a lot of the work. Dr Baron knew that with Dad's poor eating background he would need Mum to make the effort. Not everyone is as fortunate as my Dad, to have a 'personal chef' who is so good with no-fat cooking and motivation. It is, however, *more than* possible for each person who reads this book to adopt a healthy motivational attitude which will allow them to set and achieve their very own healthy body-shaping goals.

My entire family enjoyed the benefits of cutting out fat. I, for one, was trim and taut and happy to be me. The last thing on my mind was dieting. It just seemed not to be an issue any more. I figured we had this healthy living thing sewn up.

I began modelling at the age of twenty. Even though I always had a steady stream of work (mainly catwalk), I still lacked confidence. I had a serious self-image problem from all the years of yoyo dieting.

I think it's important at this point to let you know that I never weighed two-hundred-and-something pounds. The sort of weight I am talking about gaining amounts to a couple of dress sizes up and down. That is not to say that if you are more than a few sizes larger than your desired weight that this system won't work for you – *it will.*

> The majority of overweight Australians aren't obese, they are just a few sizes bigger than they'd like to be.

I have designed this system in such a way that it is as effective in dropping the odd kilo as it is in dropping the even 100 pounds.

After beginning work with Sydney's leading personal trainer, Geoff Barker, (who happened to be Commando in the top-rating *Gladiators* TV show) I learnt some interesting facts about body shaping. Because I wasn't all that excited by what I saw in the mirror, I set a new goal and I knew I couldn't (and didn't want to) starve myself to do it!

> I threw away my bathroom scales, and took out my tape measure and my favourite pair of jeans!

I did this because muscle tissue actually weighs up to three times more than fat. Because I knew I was losing fat and gaining muscle tissue, the scales would appear inaccurate, and could also make even the most motivated person feel like giving up completely. My trusty tape measure and favourite pair of jeans saved the day. Each Sunday morning before church, I would try on my favourite jeans until they fit like a comfy glove. They went from 'breathe-in-and-squeeze-and-forget-it', to 'they're-on-but-don't-ask-me-to-sit-down', to 'Wow!-what-a-babe!' *(so I was told!)* This feeling was so incredibly rewarding!

I set my goal – and I achieved it without swaying! I lost inches and felt wonderful. It took a complete focus of mind and a determination.

> I had to make choices to reach my goal.

I applied the no-fat principles, together with a healthy eating plan where I was having five small meals a day, plus walking. I fully achieved my goal.

I don't care to count the number of years I spent nearly killing myself in aerobic classes, week in, week out. It wasn't until I slowed down and took part in some *steady exercise,* at the rate my body worked best, that I saw the *fat burning* results *I wanted.*

•

Geoff is a former English body building champion. *He* knew how to get into shape. The only problem for him was retaining it. He was the original fat kid in school who ran the slowest 100-metre sprint. He was teased and laughed at, which caused him to take up body building at the ripe old age of ten. He become a champion, twice, before his twenty-first birthday.

He maintained his physique fairly well, despite his body's natural tendency to be fat.

> Everyone is different. It was obvious
> that my body's metabolism was very
> different to Geoff's.

My metabolism was damaged from lack of eating as a teenager and Geoff's from eating far too much fat as a child. We both needed to sort this problem out.

Since leaving the British Royal Marines in 1988, Geoff has been working in gyms and fitness centres as a personal trainer. He has trained some of the weirdest and most wonderful bodies in the world. His sheer determination and his insatiable desire to find out all there is to know about what makes great bodies great, has given him knowledge beyond his years. Also, his fat-boy past has given him a personal understanding which a great number of fitness instructors lack.

After studying nutrition and working closely with body-shaping gurus, Geoff became aware of a phenomenon. It was nearly as amazing as no fat, but has been kept a much bigger secret.

> If Geoff cut out all starchy carbohydrates after around 3 pm, his body would strip fat much more quickly and efficiently than any other method he'd tried.

Increasing his cardiovascular activity (walking, cycling, etc.) also aided greatly in his fight against fat. Geoff's physique changed dramatically once he adopted these few simple principles.

Geoff has taught me a lot. *No fat*, combined with *limited starchy carbs*, and some *easy exercise*, now gave us a wider scope for helping people.

Once we developed the Fat Free Forever Body Shaping System, it was simply a matter of applying it and always checking back to the reference point we knew would bring us into line, without cheating, and in the shortest amount of time. Everyone needs a system that works for them.

•

I continued modelling right up until I was three months pregnant with twin boys, Bentley and Beau. Knowing that fat cells can be laid down four times through a woman's life – early childhood, adolescence, pregnancy and menopause – I knew that if I kept my fat intake to a minimum while pregnant, I wouldn't have to work as hard afterwards. I did, however, increase my healthy eating!

By the end of my pregnancy, I had nearly reached 100 kilos and I certainly outgrew XL maternity clothes. I am now very proud to say that over just a few short months (considering that I breastfed my babies for twelve months), I am now back in shape. I also have the energy and vitality I had in my teens and, believe me, I need it with my boys!

Fat Free Forever tells you specifically WHAT to do, WHEN to do it, and HOW it should be done. And, unlike a lot of other 'diet' books, it clearly explains the most important factor – WHY.

> There's nothing as important as grasping a reason for doing something to enable you to put it into practice, *for life*!

Finding the keys to this great Body Shaping System that works has been a great learning process for me, and a combination of effort and determination, but they've paid off. After reading *Fat Free Forever: The Body Shaping System you* will also know there is *always* a point of reference to come back to – a balance – *Fat Free Forever*. Even if you're pregnant, sick, or just completely off the rails for a while with your eating, it's always there.

Life is full of choices.

If you eat often, *you will* help burn fat.

By increasing your lean protein intake, *you will* maintain muscle, and *you will* help burn fat.

Do some steady, simple exercise, and *you will* burn fat and shape up.

I've done the lot, so have our clients – and now it's *your turn!*

Welcome to the world of being *Fat Free Forever.*

I would like to thank my wonderful family for their tireless encouragement and support.

Thank you too Geoff, Eden and Selwa for having the vision and passion to see this book published.

Introduction

If someone told you there is a way to never be fat again, and it is a simple equation – you'd follow it, wouldn't you?

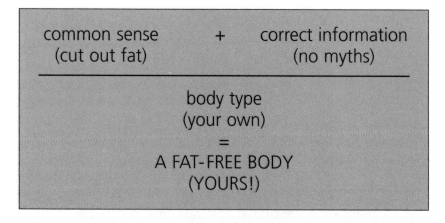

$$\frac{\text{common sense (cut out fat)} + \text{correct information (no myths)}}{\text{body type (your own)}} = \text{A FAT-FREE BODY (YOURS!)}$$

Although I am a qualified fitness leader and personal trainer, it is not the only background to this book. It's more than that. It's trial and error and experience, with my partner, Geoff Barker, family, and hundreds of clients we have been involved with over the years. After all, who ever really changed from just knowing something and not actually applying it to their life?

Our clients wanted to know *WHAT* we do, *WHEN* to do it, and *exactly HOW* it should be done. So I wrote *Fat Free Forever: The Body Shaping System* for them. Our clients are people like you and me – busy and often disheartened by countless failed attempts at dieting – who really want to be healthy, look great, and eat well, forever.

> This book is somewhat extreme!
> It uses what a lot of diet programme's
> don't use – common sense.

I am going to teach you to forget low fat and to remember no fat! After all, it's obvious that you cannot take off what you keep putting in! My theory is, if you can see the fat, it's too much. As there are enough natural fats in foods, I have designed recipes and methods around utilising this minimal amount of unseen fat in cooking. Not one recipe has any added oil, butter or cream.

I've created plenty of no-fat recipes to tempt any tastebud, lighten the load of any heart, and to shape any body. What's also unique about this book is its coding system. Each recipe is coded for the best time of day to eat a particular meal. The code is user friendly, and plays a major role in the whole Body Shaping System.

Did you know that your metabolism works more efficiently in the morning than the evening? That's why I encourage larger meals earlier, and lighter meals at night.

> It's not just what you eat
> (although this is obviously important),
> but also the time of day you eat it.

This is one of the absolute keys to getting your body into great shape, and is explained in detail throughout *Fat Free Forever*.

Anyone who's been on any type of diet will be happily surprised at the amount of food we are suggesting should be eaten each day. Often people under-eat, which causes the slowing down of their metabolism, which in turn causes the storage of body fat to increase. This is what starving to be slim can do!

The whole point of personal trainers is to provide a personal service. Obviously this can't be done through a book, so we've crossed the line. The reason this book is different from other diet books is that we've produced *Fat Free Forever* in the style of a training manual, which will enable you to adapt our principles to your lifestyle *and* make it personal to you.

It's simple once you understand it. The WHAT, WHEN, HOW and WHY of Fat Free Forever Body Shaping contained in this book are uncomplicated.

> I've included brand names to help you shop,
> coded recipes to help you cook, menu planners
> to help you eat and a Junk Day once a week,
> to help keep you sane!

What have you been eating lately? Do you eat breakfast? Do you know your proteins from your carbohydrates? Do you even care? It is positively vital that you understand your body.

Just as an instruction manual is necessary to repair a television or video, we could have done well with a Body Shaping instruction manual at birth. It's simple reality that we just don't know enough about our bodies, so we therefore can't expect a lot from them. This System can become your Body Shaping Training Manual.

> Without involvement, there's no commitment.
> Mark it down, asterisk it, circle it, underline it.
> No involvement, no commitment!
> Stephen R. Covey

You may be familiar with the Healthy Food Pyramid, or the Five Food Groups that were taught at school. What you need to do now is put them aside in your mind, in your cupboard, or even in your bin, while we explore the wonderful world of the Body Shaping Food Groups. I don't believe square pegs should have to be squeezed into round holes, so you will learn how to adapt these Fat-Free principles into YOUR BODY and YOUR LIFE. You *can* do this!

Chapter

Expect This ...

You will want to know what to expect if you follow this Body Shaping System. You will lose fat, retain muscle tissue, lower cholesterol, have increased energy, and you will sleep soundly.

> You will look and feel great and everyone will notice!

Firstly, if you follow what I've outlined, even if you cannot manage to take part in any exercise, you will lose body fat. Basically what doesn't go in your mouth – fat – has to come off your body. And what's left underneath the fat is your body's muscle tissue, which gives you your shape, so we don't want to lose it!

Because muscle outweighs fat by three times, it's important not to weigh yourself constantly. Instead, grab your favourite piece of clothing that you wish you could fit into, and try it on no more than once a week.

Also, if you can, have a personal trainer do a Fat Test on you. You will be surprised at the amount of fat lost after being on the System for a few weeks. You may not see dramatic results in weight or size loss in the first week or so, because you won't be losing water or muscle tissue, which is the bulk of the weight lost on regular diets.

The reality is that stubborn fat is always the last to leave your body.

> You will be laying down no-fat foundation stones by sticking to the System.

This means that if you go off the rails later on, you can always get back on, and it will only take you about one-third of the time to regain your great body shape.

Don't expect the same results you've had with other diets. You may even feel like giving up after a week, but once you've pushed through the ten-day mark you will be firing! It will become a part of your routine.

The body's metabolism is truly remarkable. I liken it to needing to go to the bathroom. Once your body is so in tune with proper eating, it lets you know – loud and clear – when it wants to eat. For the first week or so, you will probably have to keep checking on what to eat and when to eat it. After that, your body will yell out for it.

This System is part of an education process. I'm educating your mind; it's up to you to educate your body. This is the only way you'll change your body's metabolism into super-turbo mode!

At around the three-week mark, you will see a difference and you will certainly feel different. 'I am sleeping so soundly now', 'I have a tremendous amount of energy throughout the day'. These comments are from normal, everyday people – not even necessarily those who are able to go to the gym each day to exercise. It's simply due to proper eating.

If you cannot exercise (I know what it's like to have small kids, and how restrictive that can be), this System *will* work for you. However, by adding some steady exercise, such as walking for 45 to 60 minutes a day, three to five times a week, you will lose even more body fat.

And, if you are really keen, try to get to a gym where there are good weights machines to start sculpting your body.

•

Everyone wants to know what makes the great great. To simplify the issue, it's basically fat-free eating, limiting the amount of starchy carbohydrates (especially at night), taking part in steady exercise, such as walking, and hitting the gym to do weights about three times a week. This is an optimum plan for an optimum body.

At about the six-week mark (even without exercise), you will notice a real difference in your body's shape. This will motivate and catapult you into the next phase. I try to only set goals that are around the six-to-eight week mark – something achievable. If you know the truth of what to expect at the outset, then this training manual will not only assist your motivation, but you will not stop, because it's happening on schedule for you, and you will see great results.

> Because I've been on the receiving end of sticking to the System for six to eight weeks, the results are always enough to keep going.

Imagine setting a body-shaping goal and actually achieving it! It does wonders for your self-esteem, not to mention your body shape!

> Begin with the end in mind.
> Stephen R. Covey

Be realistic in your goal setting, and remember the old saying, 'Slow and steady wins the race'. It will work for you. Don't be in a big hurry to lose it too quickly, or else (as usual), it won't stay off.

Sit back and dream about the type of body shape you want, the size you want to be, and then you start planning for it.

Chapter

2

Establish Your Enemies

It's the war against the bulge, so it's important to establish your enemies and be ready for combat. Who are your enemies?

> 1 is Fat
> 2 is Starchy Carbohydrates in the evening,
> 3 is either Under- or Overexercising

Fat is one of the greatest body-shaping enemies – in fact it's definitely the worst, and it's important to recognise this first of all. Search it out, track it down and eliminate it.

The second lethal body-shaping enemy is consuming starchy carbohydrates – bread, pasta, rice and potatoes and, for the midnight munchers, cereal – at the wrong time of day, which is basically any time after 3 pm. These three enemies really are a combination that cause damage. Discontinuing one without the others simply will not help you achieve the body shape of your dreams.

The myth surrounding starchy carbohydrates – 'energy foods' – is that you need copious amounts of them to function each day. The only problem with this is that unless you are training like an ironman, you shouldn't be eating breakfast cereal like one! Unless you are extremely active – and 90% of us are not – then energy foods, including bananas, will be stored in your body. This unused glut of energy foods is stored in the form of fat.

Nine times out of ten, if you are feeling lethargic and needing what you think is an energy boost, your body is dehydrated and simply needs a water refuelling, and could probably do with a brisk walk around the block!

Firstly you need to assess your body type (see Body Types and Metabolism, p. 23), and only take in food that you need to function healthily, to give you enough fibre and energy to fight the fight against fat, and nothing more.

You may well be watching your fat intake and reducing your evening meal, but it's important that you realise that the 'No Fat' and the 'No Starchy Carbs in the evening' theories are what are going to make the difference to everything you've ever tried before.

The third important aspect of fat burning is to make sure that when you exercise, you take it steady and don't get breathless. Now this doesn't mean that you shouldn't work up a sweat, but it does mean that you should be working at a pace you can stick at, and not have to give up in case you keel over.

The minute you become too breathless, you will be burning carbohydrates and *not fat*. So slow down and go for longer if you can. I'll be covering why this is so important in Easy Exercise (see p. 89). Don't miss it!

There is no need to wonder now about what works and what doesn't. We've taken care of that for you in our everyday working capacity as personal trainers.

The fight against body fat is a real combination of efforts. For some examples of elimination, and of what works and what doesn't, please read on.

Example 1: one-out-of-three

You attend high-impact aerobics classes a few times a week and come home to a nice bowl of pasta or rice, with absolutely no fat. It's okay, but you're still not losing any weight.

Example 2: two-out-of-three

You attend high-impact aerobics classes a few times a week and come home to a medium-sized serving of protein and a small serving of fibrous carbohydrates (broccoli, carrots, snow peas, corn, etc.), with absolutely no fat. It's okay, but you're still losing only a little weight.

Example 3: three-out-of-three

You walk for 45–60 minutes a day, three to five times a week, and at night you eat a medium-sized serving of protein and a small serving of fibrous carbohydrates with absolutely no fat. You are finally losing weight – and it's not water or muscle, it's fat!

Chapter 3

Body Types and Metabolism

There are three body types, and most people are a mixture of two of them.

Ectomorph   naturally thin
eats anything
has difficulty keeping any weight on
often nervy and hyperactive.

Mesomorph   naturally lean
athletic build
has little problem with food.

Endomorph   naturally round
puts on weight by looking at food
has a hard time dieting.

Please don't instantly presume that you are naturally an *endomorph* just because you are trying to lose weight. Poor eating habits can push you into the 'hard-to-lose' category, but you may well be genetically one of the other types or, more likely, a mixture.

> Only your metabolism and muscles burn fat.

Your metabolism is like an engine that constantly runs, keeping your body working, burning fuel for body functions and energy. It fluctuates throughout the day, depending on certain factors, including the time of day you eat and exercise.

In the fight against fat, it's vital to keep your metabolism up as much as possible. When it slows naturally, as it does at night so you can sleep, it's important that you eat only low-energy foods so they are not stored as fat.

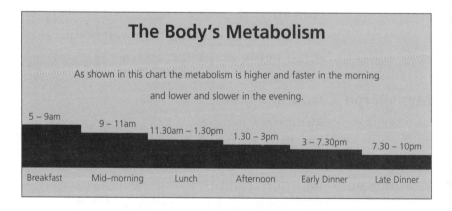

The Body's Metabolism

As shown in this chart the metabolism is higher and faster in the morning and lower and slower in the evening.

5 – 9am	9 – 11am	11.30am – 1.30pm	1.30 – 3pm	3 – 7.30pm	7.30 – 10pm
Breakfast	Mid–morning	Lunch	Afternoon	Early Dinner	Late Dinner

If your metabolism is slow from either genetics or poor eating habits, don't presume that it will never speed up.

Our best success stories have come from clients who have been overweight all of their lives, for both of the above reasons. The great news is, in a very short time, considering how long these clients have been overweight, they not only lost the weight they wanted to, but their metabolism became faster and more efficient.

Without addressing the real problem of body fat, by trying diets here and there, you are virtually putting a Band-Aid over a compounding problem. The only way to cure this problem is to change your body's metabolism once and for all. It may mean you must have more diligence in the beginning, but you can increase your body's metabolism over time, which in the long term will make life much more enjoyable.

Your body has a base metabolism of 1000 calories a day, give or take a few hundred. This is the minimum amount your body needs to burn to keep you alive. Any activity beyond this point will add to your total daily energy expenditure.

If you raise this figure by increasing your natural base metabolism through correct eating, you will see how your body will instantly burn more fat. And, if you were to add sensible metabolism-stimulating eating habits, you will see even more fat disappear. Of course, exercise will speed things up even more by stimulating your metabolism and increasing your overall consumption of energy.

This information is vital as it allows you to understand the 3 Keys to Body Shaping Success. If you keep these 3 Keys firmly in your mind whenever you eat anything, making a choice will be a lot easier.

3 KEYS

1 Instead of weighing everything on your plate, weigh it in your head.
(Am I satisfied? Do I need to eat this?)

2 Consider the effort required for your body to burn what you're about to eat.
(1 hour walk = 400 calories or a medium-sized plate of food.)

3 And, most importantly, will you have time or be motivated enough to burn what you're about to eat after you've eaten it?
(Exercise can be a great appetite suppressant!)

Chapter 4

Body-shaping Food Groups

This chapter has been designed to help you understand the different types of foods I'll be suggesting you eat, and why. Rather than listing our suggested foods in a food pyramid, I've decided to be more original (and practical), and go into much more detail. I've explained not only what to eat, but why and how it will affect your Body Shape.

If you don't particularly like the food I've suggested, or if you are allergic to it, it can, in 99% of cases, be substituted. Once you read through all the detail, you should be able to create your own Personal Body Shaping Food Pyramid.

> Remember, food can be a means to an end,
> or it can be enjoyed along the way.
> You are what you eat!

PROTEIN

Protein is a vital part of your daily eating plan. It also happens to be one of the most misunderstood areas of nutrition. The meat lobby expounds the virtues of the 'near-medicinal' qualities of various meats. Then there's the vegetarians, who propose life after hamburgers with lentils and soya beans. Finally there's the health fanatics, drinking shape-up shakes and miracle slimming drinks. So what is what, and who's right and who's wrong? These groups all have fairly sound reasons for their choice of protein intake. We, however, will go a step further to find out what is best for us in our quest for a *better body shape*.

Most people don't ask what they are eating for. By reading *Fat Free Forever*, I presume your reason is to change your body shape, so let's look at the options for eating from that particular angle. Protein is your body's building blocks. If you took all the water out of your body, you would be left with just over 50 % pure protein. Now that should give you something to think about. Your body also annually renews more than 95% of all its molecules, and every molecule is made up predominantly of protein and water. *That's how important protein is!*

Now, as impressive as that information may be, you still need to know how that relates to a better body shape. Unfortunately, most dieters forget this next very important point: muscle will only tone and shape if there is enough protein to feed it. The reason we want muscle to tone is so we will look and feel better, but, even more importantly than that is the fact that *toned muscle is incredibly efficient at burning fat.* Muscles use fat as their fuel, so the more toned and stronger the muscles, the more efficient they are at burning fat. For example, imagine a 4-cylinder car – it doesn't burn very much fuel because the cylinders are small and it is not a very powerful vehicle, but an 8-cylinder car needs many more litres of fuel because it is much more powerful. Therefore, it's obvious that by making our bodies more efficient through eating and exercising correctly, we will become more like the 8-cylinder car. We are going to turn everyday movements and activities into fat- and calorie-consuming workouts!

This is why protein consumption is so important.

In deciding which protein is best for you to eat, refer to the protein chart on p. 32 which will give you a complete guide to the best and worst proteins.

Meat Proteins

To help you better understand this section I am referring to meat proteins as any animal product, including poultry, fish and dairy products. Meat can be an excellent source of what are called 'complete proteins', which means that they contain all the eight essential amino acids in the quantities needed to be fully used by the body. If a food doesn't contain all the amino acids in the correct ratios, it is called an 'incomplete protein', because the body cannot use it all.

You don't need to know in detail which amino acids do what. It is fairly easy to remember that all meats and dairy products have the eight essential amino acids in good amounts, and that all vegetables, fruit and grains either don't have any at all, or they are substantially lacking in them.

So from this perspective, meat proteins are a good choice. Of course, as you will have read on the protein chart, some meats are a whole lot better than others because of their fat content. Generally, fish and white meat rate highest, and so should be considered before all others when choosing a protein from this category.

Vegetable Protein

As already mentioned, vegetables are not great sources of protein on their own. When it comes to consuming enough to meet your daily requirements, this can cause a problem – especially if you are exercising or are fairly active. To ensure you are getting the complete eight essential amino acids from vegetables, dried beans, peas, lentils and grains, you must eat two or more of these foods together, for example, dried beans and a grain such as brown rice or couscous.

Being a vegetarian can turn into a science of its own, learning what goes with what. At the end of the day, vegetarians will often still have consumed under the optimum daily requirements, because of the low amount of essential amino acids – gram for gram – in vegetables.

Most people know that nuts and soya beans are relatively good forms of protein. However, they are both proteins that are not readily absorbed by the body, and nuts contain huge amounts of fat! AVOID THEM.

Slimming Shakes

This is an interesting area where, unfortunately, a good idea has grown into a monster! Have you ever read the contents on the labels of these drinks? You would become slimmer drinking a melted chocolate sundae.

It is, however, very easy to distinguish the good from the bad, and it is well worth the effort to do so. Protein shakes are actually your **BEST** option for optimum results. Providing you have selected the correct kind of protein, the pros are that they are:

- a lot lower in fat than meat protein
- far more absorbable than meat or vegetable protein
- very convenient and filling.

What you should be looking for is whey protein concentrate (when wpc itself is basically the only ingredient), egg albumen and casein. They are all *low in fat* and *high in protein*. It's important to read all the ingredients on the labels, because if the shakes contain sugars, full cream, vegetable or any other oil, give them a big *fat* miss! Those containing soy protein too high on the list of ingredients are selling you a little short of useful ingredients.

In Summary

Armed with the protein chart, you should be able to make the best choices every time, now knowing the importance of choosing them. One last thing to remember: it doesn't matter how high in amino acids and how absorbable or low in cholesterol the protein is if you cover it in fat when cooking it. Think before you eat!

PROTEIN CHART

Lean Protein (Listed from best to worst)

Whey Protein Concentrate (Protein Shake)

This is the best form of protein available at present. Although it's available as one of many ingredients in a few different types of protein powders, the best form is when it's the only ingredient. It is the most readily absorbable protein available and is less than 1 per cent fat. WPC is convenient as you can mix it and take it to work, and mix it in cooking if you wish. It is also very inexpensive. The latest scientific evidence shows that whey protein boosts the body's immunity by up to 500%. It's a great natural appetite suppressant and contains properties which help speed the body's metabolism. But it is not a meal replacement, or a protein replacement; it is a natural protein.

Whey Protein Concentrate is available in all leading health food shops and supermarkets. Look for 'Life-Body Shaping Food', which is pure WPC, produced by Aussie Bodies. Please refer to page 237 for further details on where you can purchase this form of protein.

However, it's most important that you do not confuse pure WPC with ion exchange or ionised whey protein. There are some protein supplements available which contain these supposedly 'high tech' ingredients, which unfortunately, in reality, have undergone a considerable amount of chemical treatment, which removes much of the valuable calcium, as well as many of the other beneficial properties of pure WPC, including the immune boosting and cellular regeneration benefits. Pure WPC is

NOT chemically treated, and the protein structure remains as nature intended it, ready for our bodies to be nourished by it. Aussie Bodies also produce an excellent, easy to use 375 mL Tetra pack, called LITE Body Shaping Milk which is great for mid-morning or afternoon snacks and it's 99% fat free! It's WPC mixed with skim milk and flavoured naturally with either chocolate or vanilla.

Egg Albumen (Protein Shake)

This is another good form of protein. It is available in a powder mix and is fairly inexpensive. It is very absorbable and low in fat. It too is convenient, as you can mix it and take it with you to work; also you can put it in cooking if you wish.

Eggs

Eggs are a great form of protein – there is absolutely no cholesterol in the whites, which is what we recommend you eat most of. Never have more than one egg yolk per day. One egg yolk scrambled with four to six egg whites in an omelette is delicious. Simply mix with some vegies and use a Teflon frypan. Eggs are cheap and should be used often in your eating plan. In case you are wondering what to do with the unused yolks – throw them away.

White Fish

I'm referring to the fresh variety that is neither tuna nor salmon, nor any other seafood for that matter. White fish contain minimal amounts of fish oil, but more than enough for your daily fix, so you don't need to fry it in batter and oil. Check out my fish recipes in the No-Fat Recipes section (see p. 105).

Brown Fish

Brown fish is tuna and salmon, and any other type of fish which has dark flesh. It usually is a little more oily than white fish. It is, however, an excellent source of protein and is readily available – especially tinned tuna and salmon. Tuna contains the least amount of fat of the brown fish varieties. Remember, when selecting any tinned food, go for tuna in brine or spring water, not in oil. Some of the new varieties of tuna snacks available contain mayonnaise, so be careful. Pink salmon is fractionally lower in fat than red salmon.

Turkey

Turkey doesn't have to be saved for Christmas dinner – it is lower in fat than chicken! The only problem is that it may be a little harder to find than chicken. You can substitute it for the chicken in any of the Chicken Recipes.

Chicken

Chicken seems to be most people's favourite form of protein. Chicken is easy to cook in different ways, and it's great to eat hot or cold. Make sure that you only eat chicken breast, as the thighs, legs and wings contain a higher fat content. Also, ensure all traces of skin, fat and gristle are removed *before* cooking. One of our all-time favourite recipes is my Unfried Chicken Strips recipe (see p. 111). Stay away from any processed chicken, such as chicken loaf. The way chicken is cooked will determine how much fat you end up eating, so save barbecued chicken for your Junk Day.

Veal

When you're buying veal, make sure to ask your butcher if it is tender, and then ask him to trim off any fat. You will usually have to trim again, as most butchers don't think that 'that tiny bit of fat' will hurt you. We know it will! Cook it slowly and carefully. For some ideas, check out the Veal recipes (see p. 138).

Beef

Beef is high in protein, essential vitamins and minerals, including iron, but you do only need a small piece of it now and again. Include it in your weekly eating plan for variety and taste, but please limit it. It's number nine on the list, which means there are eight other leaner, lower-in-fat types of protein to go for first.

Lamb

Lamb is quite high in fat, even when it's lean. It's only included here for a change of scenery. Have a look at the Baked Lamb with Rosemary (see p. 150). If you must have a baked dinner, at least try this No-Fat recipe!

Pork

Again, I've added pork here but only for variety. It is now available much leaner than in years gone by, however even in its new, lean form, it is really still too high in fat to eat on a regular basis. Only buy the pork fillets and make sure you go over the meat for any traces of fat.

Vegetables

If you are a vegetarian and you don't eat any dairy products or eggs, then your choice of protein is limited. A combination of vegetables will get you where you want to go, if it's your only choice, but just watch the fat content of what you're eating. You can combine green vegies with grains and rice, or mushrooms with green peas, brussel sprouts, broccoli and cauliflower, or soya beans with brown rice, wheat or corn. Remember though, *there is no protein in fruit*. I've included some appetising vegetarian recipes in the No-Fat Recipes section (see p. 105). However, if you are able, do try to include whey protein and eggs in your daily eating plan.

Fatty Protein (Listed from bad to worst)

Grams of fat per 100 gram serving (in other words – % of fat)

Brawn	16.6	Lamb's fry with Bacon	32.8
Devon	18.3	Salami	33.9
Chicken loaf	18.3	Pepperoni	36.0
Bacon (grilled)	19.2	Oxtail/Beef (average)	29.3
Soya beans (dry)	20.2	Spam	30.6
Haggis	21.5	Cabanossi	31.6
Sausages (thick)	21.3	Peanuts, dry roasted	47.6
Roast pork (2 slices)	26.7	Sunflower seeds	51.3
Lamb chump chop (fatty)	28.0	Pine nuts	71.0

When I refer to fatty protein, it should be left out completely. It includes all kinds of processed meats, and many so-called health products!

CARBOHYDRATES

Carbohydrates (let's call them carbs), were thought to be fattening until not so long ago. The first thing a dieter would do is drop potatoes, pasta and bread completely from their diet. This, of course, left little of any substance to eat, and so left the poor dieter starving!

Then came the carbs revolution. 'They are okay.' The experts said they have little or no fat, and a new form of dieting was found. So then, why isn't everyone trim and taut as promised? After all, carbs don't have fats unless you add them, do they? Let's see why.

The main role of carbs in the body is as an energy source. Without them, you'd barely be able to do normal day-to-day tasks, let alone try to maintain a healthy exercise regime as well. The body specifically uses carbs when it's working anaerobically (without oxygen). For example, carbs are like fuel for the sweaty people, puffing and panting throughout a workout. Unfortunately, that's where the problem with carbs lies.

The modern dieter, who takes in plenty of low-fat carbs morning, noon and night, had better be busting a gut for hours on end to ensure all this excess fuel is burnt up. Otherwise *it will be stored as FAT*! Wouldn't you rather be busting your gut burning fat instead of carbs? (More later!)

One myth ripe for dispelling is that eating a lot of carbs will give you heaps of energy, as the advertisements for brekkie cereals would have us believe. Unless you are fit and toned, it's like putting premium fuel into an old car.

It won't really add to the performance until the engine has been tuned. And, unlike the car, we get another top-up each day, so our fuel tanks have to expand to take all the excess.

There are several different carbs, but we are mainly concerned with **fibrous** and **starchy**.

Starchy carbs are digested much quicker than fibrous carbs (crunchy vegetables and bran) so they instil a higher concentration of energy into the blood. That's why you are told to eat a banana when playing sport. Unfortunately though, *if your body cannot burn the energy there and then, it stores it.*

Check out the carbohydrate chart for the different types of starchy and fibrous carbs. Although carb foods don't contain much fat, the body is easily able to convert them into fat for storage, if they are not used.

However, carbs do play a vital role in our system.

- They reassure your body that you are not in a famine, and so stop your metabolism from slowing down.
- They fill you up.
- They contain vital vitamins and minerals.
- They help provide energy for good training and energetic living.
- They contain most of the roughage required in your diet.

As you can see, they are a powerful weapon for healthy living, but must be handled with a lot of thought and care.

The best way to enjoy the benefits of carbs has been explained in Body Types and Metabolism (see p. 23). If necessary, give it another read, so that it's clear.

Starchy and fibrous carbs are known as complex carbohydrates. A third carbohydrate is sugar carbs, known as simple carbohydrates. Simple carbohydrates are usually refined or processed food, as opposed to the more raw or unprocessed complex carbohydrates. They are digested very quickly into the system, and release large amounts of glucose into the body – hence the sugar rush from eating a chocolate bar.

> The problem with simple carbs is that you must consume that amount of energy, or else it will be stored!

Fibrous carbs are a vital part of any diet, as well as healthy living. Fortunately, fibrous carbs can be eaten all day, in filling amounts, thus aiding good internal health on your way to a great external shape.

Although in the carbohydrate chart I have referred to suggested amounts of each starchy carbohydrate to eat each day, this is only a suggestion. You will be the best judge of what your body needs each day. If you find that your results are too slow, maybe it's time to cut back a little more on your starchy carb intake. It's impossible for us to prescribe exactly what you need, as everyone is different. You will become the best judge in time.

CARBOHYDRATES CHART

Starchy Carbohydrates (In no particular order)

> These are important in you daily eating plan.
> The amounts you eat and the time of day you eat
> them, will help determine your body's shape.

Cereal

Your breakfast shouldn't be wasted on eating cardboard – no matter how low in fat the cardboard is! You should eat something which is high in fibre and filling, such as oats made with skim milk, or Vita Brits. If you don't like either of these, then Special K or something similar is all right. If you have a favourite low-fat cereal which happens to be high in sugar, use it just as a topping over your Weetbix. Be careful: even though some cereals, including muesli, are 97–8% fat free, these figures are provided on a very small amount. You have to make choices which will help determine your body shape, so read the packets and be wary.

Pasta

Nearly everyone eats pasta. It can be enjoyed in many different ways – although for a great body shape, we suggest you steer away from traditional Italian dishes loaded with olive oil. Make up your own recipes, or check out the variety listed in the No-Fat Recipes section (see p. 105). Limit your intake of pasta though, as it does take a substantial amount of activity to use it all up. If pasta is part of your lunch, eat around one cup of cooked pasta, maximum. Pasta encompasses all different types of noodles, including instant.

Rice

Rice is easy to cook and is great with any meat or vegies. Although brown rice is fractionally higher in fat than white rice, it is a better choice. It has more fibre, is more difficult for your body to absorb, and more likely to be burned off. If you really cannot stand anything but white rice, then eat it. It's more important that you choose what you will actually stick to. There are some great fragrant rices on the market, such as jasmine. Remember, you don't need a lot for energy – a little will take you a long way. Don't forget, even rice noodles, although low in fat, are considered starchy carbohydrates.

Potatoes

You are probably thinking, 'What's dinner with no potatoes?' It's a better body shape – that's what it is! Although low in fat themselves, potatoes are starchy and stored easily by the body unless you are quite active. Jacket potatoes cooked in a hot oven without oil are great, or jammed with finely chopped vegies and strips of chargrilled chicken breast. Eat and enjoy them, but just make sure you limit them. If you were having them with your lunch, only have one medium-sized, or a couple of smaller-sized potatoes.

Bread

We've been told in recent times that bread is fine, it's just what you put on it that's potentially not! That's true enough, but too much bread can make a difference when you're trying hard to get into shape. Limit your bread intake to around two pieces per day. Go for the normal-sized bread, not the super-duper-can't-fit-in-the-toasted-sized bread. Wholegrain breads contain more fibre and, similarly to brown rice, are going to aid your metabolism speeding up. If you must eat white bread, go for the newer variety of 'wonder' bread which is white, but very high in fibre. Bread includes anything made of flour – muffins, scones, pastries, rolls, pancakes, pikelets, etc.

Fibrous Carbohydrates (Listed from best to worst)

Fruit

You can eat any fruit, except limit bananas as they are fairly high in sugars and carbs. You'd need to train like Haley Lewis before burning them off! Eat a couple of pieces of fruit each day, but try not to have any at night, when your metabolism is working at its slowest. Stay away from fruit juices, even if they are 100% fruit, because they are very high in fruit sugars. A diluted glass once in a while is okay, but certainly not daily. Water is always your staple drink for a great body. Limit your intake of dried fruits because you tend to eat more of them. Certainly don't get caught thinking that dry mixes from the health food shop are going to be good for you. They are loaded with nuts, natural sugars and fat.

Vegetables

All vegies are great, except avocado which, although low in cholesterol, is really high in fat. It just won't get you where you want to go in the fastest possible way. When you know what your starchy carbs are, you will become more inventive with your fibrous carbs. Vegetables such as carrots, celery, cucumber, green beans and lettuce can literally be grazed on all day. When eaten with plenty of water, they actually work as 'negative vegetables', meaning they burn more calories and fat than they contain themselves! They're excellent for snack attacks. Try to only lightly cook your vegies. The crunchier they are, the more fat they can help you burn. And don't cook them with any oil, not even cooking spray – ever!

FATS

> There is no such thing as low-fat fat!

Fats are very misunderstood.

Like most other areas of nutrition, scientists discover something about new fats every few months. However, we really need to be sure that we have the best information available with regards to fats, because what we do with them will make an *enormous* difference to our body's shape.

Let's look at the three types of fats.

Saturated Fats

Are really bad heart attack material. These are dripping, lard, butter, and vegetable oil.

Polyunsaturated Fats

Are low in cholesterol, and sold to make you feel good! They contain the same nine calories per gram as saturated fats. These are most margarines, even light, low, cholesterol free.

Monounsaturated Fats

Are sold as healthy, until you start trying to believe that you won't actually get fat from eating fat – *wrong*! They also contain the same nine calories per gram as saturated and polyunsaturated fats. These are olive oils.

What's good about fat?

The body needs fat for protection of its organs. It also needs fat as an energy source for aerobic activity. At this point, I'd like to explain the difference between aerobic and anaerobic activity, so you can better understand the fat-burning process.

Aerobic Activity

Believe it or not, aerobic activity is not jumping around in an aerobics class at your local gym, nearly killing yourself because of the lack of oxygen your body is suffering from. It is *steady* exercise, such as walking or cycling. As a result of taking part in steady aerobic exercise each day, *your body will burn fat*.

Anaerobic Activity

This is the type of activity that has caused many people to give up exercising completely. It should be left to the fitness fanatic. Most people are not fit enough to benefit from taking part in high-impact aerobics classes. There will be more on this very interesting topic in the Easy Exercise for Optimum Results section (see p.89). When you are breathless, your body is unable to burn fat, as it requires oxygen to do the job!

So, fat is fat, *or is it*? For the benefit of a better body, *yes it is*. For technical boffins, recent studies suggest that monounsaturated fats are slightly less likely to be stored directly as a fat cell than the dreaded killer, obese-making saturated fats.

There is a great deal more fats in food than you may think. For example, chicken drumsticks, soya beans and Atlantic salmon, just to name a few. So, to add even more fat in cooking is asking for trouble.

> Beware of so-called 'healthy' foods containing saturated fats, such as vegetable or coconut oil.

To be healthy, it is important that your body contains some fat. But take a good look in the mirror. It probably looks as though your fat stores won't run out for a while!

Your Daily Menu Planner (see p. 64), which I am suggesting you follow, contains around 20 grams of unseen fat. By unseen fat, I mean fat in an egg yolk, fat in skim milk, fat in low-fat yoghurt, fat in really lean meat, and fat in fish oil, from fish. This minimal amount of unseen fat is plenty to live on, so don't be surprised when I say you should positively, absolutely, not add any more!

If you eat 35 or 40 grams of fat in one meal (which is *easy* to do), for example, one serving of pasta carbonara, or half a family-sized block of dark chocolate, it will take up to one hour of solid aerobic walking (that's the steady, fat-burning pace), just to return to what you were before you ate it! Knowing how lethal fat is in the battle for a great body shape, it's my strongest hope and desire that you will just *leave it out*!

Fat fact Even the skinniest person has enough unseen body fat to last them on a run from Sydney to Melbourne.

DAIRY PRODUCTS

Dairy products are in a category of their own because they contain a good mix of the three other categories: proteins, carbohydrates and fats. They can be the best in protein to the worst in fat!

> Your body shape is generally a product
> of what goes in your mouth!

So many people have given up dairy products because they believe doing so will make them healthy, and it seems almost trendy to do so at the moment. Lactose intolerance has become a phase. Unfortunately, though, a great number of people are cutting out dairy products for *no real reason.*

> Dairy products can be your best friend
> in the fight against fat!

Low-fat dairy products are God's gift to a great body shape – and nothing short of! A low-fat, sugarless yoghurt can make your day much more bearable when you crave junk food, and can be eaten *any time of day.*

Because of the high-fat content of cheese, it's best avoided. Even the low-fat brands contain more than a desirable level of fat. Always read labels carefully and if you must eat a cheese, choose wisely and eat in strict moderation.

Skim milk can be turned into a fruit smoothy delight. It too can be drunk *any time of day*. It is a great protein and very low in carbohydrate and fat.

If you don't particularly like the taste of the fresh skim milk available, try the UHT variety. It is full-bodied, tastes creamy and one of the best things about it is that you can buy a dozen at a time and store them.

If you feel that you are, or may be, lactose intolerant, try taking in small amounts of dairy products (with the okay from your doctor first, of course), as this may slowly stimulate the enzymes you need to tolerate lactose in your body. Alternatively, pineapple is a good enzyme.

One of the greatest benefits of consuming plenty of dairy products, especially for women, is the amount of calcium they supply each day. It's frightening that we've consulted so many female clients who have cut out nearly all dairy products for fear that they would make them fat – or even more simply because they didn't like them. These women become dangerously deficient in calcium.

Chapter 5

Water and Other Drinks

Most of us are aware that we should drink water. Few people, however, realise how vitally important it is to our well-being. To give you some idea of how much water is contained in your body, have a look at these statistics:

Lungs:	90%
Blood:	82%
Brain:	76%
Bones:	25%

Many people suffer from lethargy and tiredness in the afternoon. However, in nine out of ten cases, it's not sugar or carbohydrate energy that's lacking, it's the effects of dehydration!

Water is best absorbed by your body plain. Drinks such as tea, coffee and alcohol actually cause dehydration, so the more of these you drink, the more water you should consume. For example, for every cup of tea I drink, I try to have two extra cups of water on top of my daily water requirements.

What are the daily water requirements? Current wisdom says eight glasses a day – but how big is a glass? We are recommending that you drink at least one and a half litres of (preferably bottled or filtered) water each day. If you're not sure of this amount, keep an old drink bottle and refill it each morning.

You'll be surprised how easy it is when it becomes part of your daily routine. The more water you drink, the more thirsty for water you become.

Flavoured drinks can't be considered plain water, as flavoured liquids will often be digested differently. Add a squeeze of fresh lemon juice if you need it. Remember, some flavoured drinks can dehydrate, so be sure you reach your one and a half litre quota of plain water each day, minimum.

Tap water these days is far from beneficial to your health – especially if you are drinking several litres of it. The chemicals which are added to clean it are quite toxic, and too many of them can be cumulative.

> Your number one choice should be purified or distilled water.

A lot of mineral waters are as bad, or worse, than tap water, and can contain several chemicals – most of which are untreated. I'm not saying that it's going to make you ill, it's just that for well-being and body function, wouldn't you prefer 80% of your body to be consist of clean water, with minimum amounts of heavy metals, pesticides, chemicals and carcinogens?

Don't kid yourself that mineral water is going to provide any great amount of useful minerals. The content is so minute, that to drink distilled water (the cleanest type), will make literally no difference to your daily mineral intake.

I recently had a water filter put into my sink at home, which has cut the expense of buying bottles and bottles and bottles of distilled water! There are less expensive methods of filtering water; check with your local health food shop for the most up-to-date product information.

> Sports drinks are *very* over-rated, and one of the big traps for body shapers.

Good intentions can lead to the consumption of several hundred calories you simply do not need. If you are over-doing getting fit, or training for an event, then a fluid replacer, or electrolyte, can help a lot. *But* if you are burning fat at optimum levels, then water is more than adequate for rehydration.

Alcohol is high in calories and is best kept for use in moderation for your Junk Day.

If you feel that you can't get enough energy for that early-morning walk, a good old faithful cuppa coffee or tea (with skim milk) will serve well in giving you a boost, which also helps raise your metabolism without any excess fat or sugar. For a pick-me-up, diet colas are another form of caffeine which you can drink. I don't recommend that you go crazy with these drinks. Use them sparingly. That way, they will work a lot better, as your body doesn't become accustomed to the artificial stimulation.

Chapter 6

Vitamins

This can be a sensitive topic that people become very passionate about, especially with regards to their preferred vitamins. So often we've heard people say, 'I get all the vitamins I need from food'. The unfortunate reality is that this is extremely unlikely for the average person because of pollution, toxins, fast living, stress, lack of exercise, overexercise, or simply because of the poor nutrients in the food most people eat.

Most processed, mass-produced food is treated, refined, stored, preserved, irradiated, frozen, force-fed, chemically enhanced, and/or grown in industrially polluted farm soils with cheap, nutritionally empty fertilisers that produce a lot of empty, water-filled produce.

Sounds appetising, doesn't it? Just one of these factors is more than enough to totally ruin the nutritional quality of food, and if it doesn't, there is always the way we cook and store the food at home that will really finish off the job!

The Government's Recommended Daily Allowance

(RDA) is based on data designed to provide the minimum amount of a nutrient needed to prevent certain diseases, such as scurvy. It was initially established for the average person from a time when life was less stressful. The minimum requirement isn't able to diagnose any of your individual vitamin requirements, to know the quality of the food you eat, or how your particular body assimilates food.

This information may appear critical, and certainly is open to controversy, but the average diet doesn't hold much nutrition at all, and a dieting diet usually contains even less.

Although throughout Your Daily Menu Planner (see p. 64) and No-Fat Recipes we are suggesting you eat plenty of fresh fruit, vegetables, dairy products, fish and lean meats, it's important to realise that even the freshest of foods are often subject to inadequate growing, storage and handling these days.

So, to prevent illness and to ensure maximum health and performance of your body (and that includes your ability to burn fat and shape up), I suggest a few simple vitamins to include daily.

Vitamin C

Vitamin C is vital for the production of collagen, which is the cement which binds just about your whole body. It helps to build the immune system and protects against antioxidants which cause old age, as well as helping to repair the body after a hard day. The minimum amount taken per day should be 1000 to 2000 mg. An orange contains 10 mg, so you can see how many of them you'd have to eat! If you feel run down or as though you may be coming down with something, double the dose, or even treble it. It's important that you take vitamin C before you get sick, as it works far better as a preventative medicine than it does a cure.

Vitamin B Complex

Vitamin B complex is the commando of the B group of vitamins. It's great against stress. If you're feeling run down, take one or two each day, depending on the type and what the bottle label says.

Multivitamins

It is very important to purchase a good-quality multivitamin. A lot of vitamins can be bought quite cheaply, but what most people don't realise is that you really do get what you pay for. The cheaper vitamins are usually the least absorbable and are low doses, so you need to take more. Go for quality, as this ensures that you are not missing anything important in your diet. Ask at your local health food shop or chemist if you aren't sure about what's best for you.

Calcium

I would like to think that by now most people are aware of the absolute importance of calcium, especially women. Unfortunately, most women, and nearly as many men, are calcium deficient, and don't even make the minimum

RDA! The so-called calcium-rich dairy products contain calcium that is only about 20% absorbable.

The 800 mg RDA that you think you are getting from your two glasses of full-cream milk is only giving you 170–200 mg of useable calcium, which leaves you 600 mg short of the RDA. As you can see, good supplements can be useful. Again, be aware that many calcium supplements are not well absorbed and therefore are a waste of money. Calcium carbonate is the most absorbable.

Iron

A great many women have found that they are iron deficient. This is another example of poor modern living. An iron supplement is a lot lower in fat than a piece of lean red meat, although eating a piece of steak once a week is not a bad thing. Iron is responsible for carrying oxygen in the blood, so you can see that since the brain and muscles need oxygen to work, iron is vital. Coffee and tea can actually block the absorption, so this is another great reason to supplement your iron intake.

Chapter 7

Q & A of What and Why

WHAT ABOUT CELLULITE?

Cellulite is fatty deposits in the body, and not toxins blocking fat, or anything else. The only way to get rid of cellulite is to get rid of the fat and exercising. You can do this by following this System. It all comes down to what you eat, when you eat it, and how much exercise you do. There is no magic lotion or potion to eliminate cellulite. I had it, and I got rid of it by following this System.

WHAT ABOUT SUGAR?

I'm sure by now you're wondering why we have hardly yet mentioned sugar. It's mainly because it's not a big issue. That's not to say that you should eat tonnes of it, but fat is a far greater food enemy. Although sugar does not contain fat, if it's not burned it will be stored as fat, so use it in moderation. Don't have it in your tea and coffee, but don't worry about it if it's in sauces in small amounts. Sugar substitutes such as artificial sweeteners or honey are alternatives, but eat them in moderation as well. Be careful you read the labels on everything. Sugar and fat together can be a disastrous body-shaping combination!

WHAT ABOUT SALT?

Salt won't make you fat or thin, so decide on taste. I'm not preaching health here, just body shaping. Because it contains no calories, and of course no fat, salt is helpful to use in cooking. If you have high blood pressure or some other condition so that your doctor has limited your salt intake – then listen to your doctor. When you are using salt, always add it in moderation.

WHAT ABOUT CHOCOLATE?

As you will read in the Junk Food Chart (see p. 73), chocolate is way up there with the worst of them. This is mainly because of its fat rather than sugar content. Don't be fooled – carob is just as bad. So, save it for Junk Day. One tip though: if you have a sweet tooth and crave something, go for a couple of jubes or jelly beans instead of chocolate; at least they don't contain fat. If you are really craving sugar, especially later in the day, this is usually because you haven't eaten enough carbs earlier. There are a few really good, low-fat (97–8% fat free) chocolate ice-creams on the market. Limit these, as you will tend to overeat their recommended serving size, which means you'll end up eating loads more grams of fat than you thought.

WHAT ABOUT PREGNANCY?

It's really important that you don't do anything radical when pregnant. Take it from someone who knows. You need to eat plenty of fresh foods, but there is absolutely no reason why you shouldn't follow this System. I did, this and I gave birth to healthy-sized twins. The main point to remember is that you are the best and only judge of the amount of food you need. Just stick with the principles. I found it incredibly hard to exercise throughout my pregnancy, but I do recommend you walk every day. You'll need this added energy when Junior comes along!

WHAT ABOUT BREASTFEEDING?

Even the head lactation consultant at the hospital advised me that I only needed to drink water to produce breast milk. Providing you are eating plenty of dairy products (low-fat, of course), and lots of fresh fruit, vegetables, grains, eggs and lean meat, not only will your doctor be satisfied, but you and your baby will be too. Just keep to the principles of the System. I found that I didn't lose most of my weight during breastfeeding – it seemed to pour off a month or two afterwards. I attribute this to being careful throughout the pregnancy and feeding periods.

Section

2

When and Why

Chapter 8

Timing Your Meals

Your body's energy levels vary throughout the day. Rather than depriving your body of necessary foods that may be considered heavy, such as starchy carbohydrates, we have worked out a schedule which enables you to eat plenty of nutritious foods, it's just that they're probably in a different order to what has been normal for you.

This is an area of habit replacement which will prove vital to improving your body's shape. Making correct choices will give you the results you're after.

> You can't talk your way out of problems you've behaved yourself into.
> Stephen R. Covey

In the following pages of Your Daily Menu Planner, you'll see that at the top of each page is a box containing essential information on the type of food you should be eating at that meal and the time of day you should eat it.

It's important to understand that Your Daily Menu Planner has been designed to help you, so use our guidelines, but feel free to adapt them to your lifestyle. So you know the boundaries: you cannot change the type of food to eat at each meal, but you can change the timings within a half-hour flexibility radius.

This means that if it's 11.30 am and you haven't had your mid-morning snack, then make sure you still eat it – but have it before noon. Then, because you're running a little late, have your lunch at the later end of the scale, and get back on track ready for your afternoon snack.

Once you learn this System, it's easy. Your body actually does the learning for you. It will let you know that it needs a meal or a snack, and when you check your watch, you'll realise that it always yells out right on time.

Chapter 9

Your Daily Menu Planner

The different foods listed on the following pages are simply suggestions that have worked well for me. If you can find suitable alternatives, go right ahead, but remember to watch the fat content of anything you include. Keep the amounts medium-sized. If you feel you're not getting the results fast enough, cut back a little. If you feel as though you could eat a horse at the end of the day, then increase a little. It's important to find your own balance – it's a personal thing.

Use only Teflon (or similar) non-stick pans, and *never* use cooking sprays. They are *FAT*! And remember: don't add butter, margarine, mayonnaise, cream, oil or sugar. And watch the amount of starchy carbs you eat each day.

> Learn from the past and put it behind you.
> Look to the future and grasp it with both hands.

BREAKFAST

> ## Eat a medium serving of Starchy Carbohydrates between 5 and 9 am

2–3 Vita Brits or Weetbix
a sprinkle of bran
1 cup of skim milk
6 prunes
2 tablespoons low-fat yoghurt
1 dessertspoon honey
1 1/2 cups puffed wheat
or Special K with 1 cup skim milk and
1/2 cup of Weight Watcher's peaches

Start with 300 mL of water, then you can have tea or coffee with your breakfast. Don't drink any fruit juice as it's high in sugar.

You will not necessarily feel really full after eating this meal. Your mid-morning snack is just around the corner, so pace yourself and you will be full enough in time. Breakfast kick-starts your metabolism for the day and will help in burning fat and raising blood-sugar levels, increasing your general energy.

MID-MORNING SNACK

> Eat a small serving of Protein with a very
> small serving of Fibrous and/or Starchy
> Carbohydrates between 9 and 11.30 am

3 eggs (3 whites, 1 yolk), scrambled and cooked in a
pan, served on 1 piece of unbuttered toast
or 250 mL protein shake (see p. 113)
or 1 x 375 mL LITE WPC Tetra
or half a 'Life-Trim Snack'
or 200 grams Danone Diet Lite flavoured yoghurt and
2 rice cakes with Vegemite (no butter!)

Drink 300 mL water first, then you can have tea or coffee with your snack. If you like, you can have a diet soft drink instead of the tea or coffee, but *not* instead of the water!

After a couple of days, you will crave this snack. It's part of breakfast and part of lunch. It puts you into grazing mode, which keeps your metabolism on fire, and this helps again in burning fat. The most amazing part of this snack is if you miss it. By 5 or 6 pm, you will know it! If you have cravings at that time of day, which is normal for most people, it's because you have missed this snack, or your afternoon snack.

LUNCH

Eat a medium serving of Protein with a medium serving of Starchy and Fibrous Carbohydrates between 11.30 am and 1.30 pm

1 sandwich containing chicken breast fillet, or tuna in brine, with lettuce, carrots, tomato, beetroot and onion (no butter, margarine or mayo)

or a no-fat pasta (or any other recommended Lunch recipe from this book), or a jacket potato cooked in the microwave or oven with shredded chicken breast fillet and salad, or tuna in brine and salad.

Drink 300 mL water first, then eat.

Your lunch will become the focus of your day, just as your dinner has been in the past as it has become the main meal of the day. Make the absolute most of this meal, because for the rest of the day the meals become smaller and smaller!

AFTERNOON SNACK

Eat a small serving of Protein with a very
small serving of Starchy and/or Fibrous
Carbohydrates between 1.30 and 3 pm

200 grams Danone Diet Lite flavoured yoghurt, and
an apple or two Kiwifruit
or half a 'Life-Trim Snack'
or 1 x 375 mL LITE WPC Tetra
or 250 mL protein shake and
2 rice cakes with Vegemite (no butter!)

Drink 300 mL water first, then you can have tea or coffee with your snack, or a diet soft drink instead of the tea or coffee.

Again, after a couple of days, you will actually crave this meal. It's part of lunch and part of dinner, in the grazing mode. If you miss this important meal, you will definitely feel it around 6 to 8 pm!

STOP!

HOLD IT RIGHT HERE!

PLEASE READ THIS
BEFORE WE GO ANY FURTHER

Because your body's metabolism slows down later in the day so you can sleep at night, the later in the day you eat, the more careful you must become in your selection of food.

To help you, we have actually split dinner into two sections, depending on whether you eat early *or* late.

Remember that it's *either* early *or* late dinner, *not both*!

EARLY DINNER

> Eat a medium serving of Protein with a small
> serving of Fibrous Carbohydrates
> (no starchy carbs!) between 3 and 7.30 pm

> 1 serving of lean meat (no oil!), with lightly-steamed
> broccoli, carrots, corn, etc. followed by 200 grams
> Fruche Light
> *or* 500 mL protein shake, and
> a crunchy salad with no-oil dressing
> followed by 200 grams Danone Diet Lite yoghurt

Drink 300 mL water first, then eat. You can then have a
cup of tea or coffee afterwards.

The earlier you eat this meal the better. For absolutely
optimum results in the shortest amount of time (without
cheating), have the protein shake and salad for dinner
each night, whether it's early or late. Try it and see how
you go. You will *definitely* like the results! Ensure you go
for variety, and don't let yourself become bored! Save
the dessert recipes listed in the No-Fat Recipes section
(see p. 105) for Junk Day.

LATE DINNER

Eat a small serving of Protein ONLY between
7.30 and 10 pm

325 mL protein shake followed by 200 grams Fruche
Light

or 4 eggs (1 yolk only), scrambled, with a sprinkle of
Maggi Seasoning on top (no toast, and no butter or
margarine in eggs) followed by 200 grams Danone
Diet Lite yoghurt

Drink 300 mL water first, then eat. You can then have a
cup of tea or coffee afterwards.

What you eat for this meal is crucial. Again, for
absolutely optimum results in the shortest amount of
time (without cheating), have the protein shake as your
first choice. The great thing with the protein shake is that
you can mix it in the morning and take it with you if you
are going to be out late – and you don't have to think
twice about what to eat for this important meal.

If you're prone to the midnight munchies, relax – this
will go away. Try a small glass of skim milk instead, until
your body gets used to your new routine.

Chapter 10

Junk Day!

THE DAY YOU'VE BEEN WAITING FOR

For being so very good and sticking with the System, you can have one junk day each week – maximum. This means you can have anything from pizza to pasta with cream, or fried chicken and a chocolate sundae.

One tip though: try to keep it to one meal per week, rather than all day for the best results! ENJOY!!

JUNK FOOD CHART
(Listed from medium to bad)

	grams of fat per serve	calories per serve
Barbecued chicken (no skin)	8	190
Tasty cheese (30g)	10	120
Toasted muesli (60g)	11	267
Ice-cream, regular (1 scoop)	11	165
Milk chocolate (small block)	14	263
Pizza	15	340
Fruit muffin	16	296
Beef curry	17	344
Cheesecake (100g)	19	315
Thai noodles (100g)	20	285
Regular-sized hot chips	20	329
Hot dog	20	370
Sausage roll	22	378
Lasagne	24	546
Avocado dip (quarter cup)	24	250

JUNK FOOD CHART *(Continued)*
(Listed from bad to worst)

	grams of fat per serve	calories per serve
Quiche Lorraine	25	360
Fish and chips	28	500
Pork ribs	30	400
Spinach and cheese filo triangle (large)	30	400
Fried chicken (2 pieces)	30	410+
Meat pie	30	500
Hamburger (with the lot)	30	500+
Cadbury's Dairy Milk Chocolate (100g)	30	525
Toblerone (100g)	31	544
Banana split with cream and ice-cream	32	600
Poppy seeds (half-cup)	33	338
Flaky pastry (100g)	37	556
Chocolate-coated almonds (12–14 nuts)	44	568
Butter/Margarine (62.5g)	50	450
Eggs Benedict (2 eggs)	53	700

WHAT IS JUNK DAY?

With all the hard work that goes with dieting, we've provided you with some release. It's JUNK DAY, one day per week. Having a JUNK DAY each week not only keeps you sane and makes the days in each week pass quickly, but it actually aids in speeding up your metabolism.

The body doesn't know what's hitting it when you eat fat after being so good all week, so your metabolism goes into overdrive. It actually works for you, providing, of course, you go straight back to the System the next day!

> Whatever is at the centre of your life will be the source of your security, guidance and wisdom.
> Don't let it be food!

There's obviously varying degrees of damage you can do on your Junk Day. That's why I've listed a Bad to Worst of food you can eat in a Junk Day chart, to help you make somewhat healthier choices – if you want. You will find that you don't have to go all out to become satisfied. A little goes a long way, especially when your body is *not* used to it!

Chapter 11

Q & A of When and Why

WHEN WILL I SEE RESULTS?

You will start to feel different from two to three weeks, and begin to look different from three to five weeks. The most dramatic results will come between six and eight weeks. This is when it will show not only in your physique, but in your face. People will ask you, 'What's different?', just as they would if you'd had a haircut. You won't look drawn and tired. You will have a greater energy level, and because you'll be sleeping better (a positive side-effect of this System), you will be literally bright-eyed and bushy-tailed! The results will just keep on keeping on, for as long as you want. You may decide to be very careful for up to twelve weeks, then relax a little for the next week or two, then go back on for another four to six weeks. It can be in as many stages as you want.

WHEN SHOULD I EAT IN RELATION TO EXERCISING?

It's best not to eat just before exercising, whether it be walking or weights. The best time is to eat within half an hour of completing your daily exercise. Because your metabolism will have increased, it will ensure greater use of the refuelling.

WHEN CAN I DRINK ALCOHOL?

Coffee liqueurs and cream cocktails contain, on average, 18 grams of fat, so if you must have one, save it for Junk Day. Because of the high sugar level in other alcoholic beverages, you should also drink them, in moderation, once a week. Although red and white wine, and beer don't contain fat, they all contain enough calories in simple carbohydrates (sugar) to be stored in your body as fat. A little red wine is probably good for your health, but we suggest you don't drink it on a daily basis. Remember, what's sometimes healthy isn't necessarily going to get you into shape. In this instance especially!

WHEN CAN I WEIGH MYSELF?

You would have noticed by now that we don't ask you to weigh yourself, and it's for a very good reason. As I've said before, because muscle weighs three times more than fat, you aren't going to get a true picture of how well you're really doing on the System if you're constantly checking for dropped kilos, instead of checking for dropped inches. By all means, weigh yourself, but please, don't become obsessed with it.

WHEN'S THE BEST TIME FOR JUNK DAY?

This is a personal thing, depending on your lifestyle. I really enjoy having my Junk Day on Sundays, unless I'm entertaining on a Saturday night, then I go for No Fat Recipes, and may include a few starchy carbs, dessert and wine. If you find that, due to circumstances, you need to have two Junk Days in one week, then just be extra careful for the following ten days or so. You know the principles and you know the balance. Often on a Sunday, I come home from church and we go somewhere nice for lunch, or sit in the park with barbecued chicken and chips. It's actually better, if you have a choice, to have junk for lunch instead of dinner. At least then your body has the rest of the afternoon to try to get rid of it! Number 1 rule though – ENJOY your Junk Day!

WHEN CAN I EAT FAT AGAIN?

You will find that after you've been following the System for a few weeks it will become easy to live without added fats. Your Junk Days will probably become healthier than the food you're eating currently. Your body won't crave fat, and you'll find that when you do eat it, it makes you feel sluggish and ill.

Section

3

How
and Why

Chapter 12

Motivation

The average dieter stays on a diet for approximately three weeks. What happens after that? Usually, because they have deprived themselves so much, they end up eating far in excess of what they were eating before, just to balance what they have missed out on. Can you relate to this so far?

That's normal for dieters, but abnormal for you now. By following this system you have fallen out of the dieter category. CONGRATULATIONS!

Now the key to getting this System to work for you, is to establish goals and reach benchmarks. Your long-term goal, the end result, realistically may take some time, but to achieve your first benchmark will only take approximately six to eight weeks. Following, I've listed some easy steps to help you establish your long-term goal and to achieve your short-term benchmarks.

ESTABLISH YOUR LONG-TERM GOAL

1   You must have a dream, so start to dream if you don't have one already. *Begin with the end in mind.* Imagine the body you want to achieve. Put doubts that aren't part of the plan out of your mind, and keep a focus on what your plan is.

2   Find a photograph or clipping from a magazine which is close to the body shape you want and put it on your fridge.

3   Tell one person what you are doing and become accountable to them.

4   Realise that what has taken you years to accumulate will take time and determination to lose and keep off.

5   Make a conscious choice that you aren't going to let your tastebuds rule your life any more!

YOUR FIRST WEEK

1   Grab your favourite pair of jeans or a skirt (or similar) that's one size too small, and choose one morning each week to try them on.

2   Measure yourself with a tape measure (or have someone else do it for you). Always measure at the biggest point.

3   Remember, Junk Day is always just around the corner! Keep this at the forefront of your mind should you contemplate breaking the System.

4   Exercise as much as you can – ideally an hour's walk a day is great, along with any time you can put in at the gym or at home doing weights.

5   Only have the types of food in your house that you are allowed to eat and none other. Enjoy your Junk Day out and don't bring home any leftovers!

REACHING YOUR SECOND AND SUBSEQUENT BENCHMARKS

1   The results you achieve will be your best motivation. Stick with it and watch! You will be eating and sleeping better, you will have more energy, and people will notice how much better you're looking. You will have a glow about you that you just don't get with dieting.

2   Measure yourself with a tape measure even less often. Try to do it just once a month. And, if you wish, jump on the scales – but remember muscle weighs three times more than fat!

3   Grab the next article of clothing you want to fit into and use it for the now once a fortnight try-on.

4   Your clear skin and feeling of renewed energy will also be something which will help you continue, and will also enable you to do more exercise.

5   Your new lifestyle of eating without added fats will be something you will be used to by now. As soon as high doses of fats and sugars hit your system for Junk Day, you'll really feel it!

Your long-term body-shaping goal will determine how many benchmarks you need to set yourself. Only set them one at a time, however, and remember, *you are only human* when setting them.

> Competing with others is sport – competing with yourself is the true test.

The trick for me has been to keep the benchmarks short and sweet (so to speak!). I need to have a reason to walk for an hour a day, whether it be running errands for our business, or picking up my niece Sarah from school. I need to know that at the end of the benchmark, I am going out to dinner somewhere really special, or I'm buying some new clothes. I guess it's only human to feel that you need to know you will receive a reward at the end of it all.

The key to all this is that the reward should come from you. You arrange it and you deliver it, and know that you've done it for yourself and not because someone who'll never understand how hard it's been for you up until now, tells you to do it. Actually achieving your *new, improved body shape* possibly seems like a dream at this stage. Follow the System and soon it will become reality for you.

To retain your *new, improved body shape* you will still need to be quite careful with your eating. The wonderful news is that your metabolism will be faster and you will be able to include a few more bits and pieces of foods you really love.

If you feel yourself slipping, though, you know how you reached your goal, and you simply need to reapply those same principles.

> It's about habit replacement, creating new exciting routines, and making choices.

Fat Free Forever has been designed in every way to make getting into shape as efficient and trouble-free as possible. We offer our personal training clients the 100%, most efficient methods to reach their goals. Out of that 100%, it's really up to you just how much you decide to do. At least you will have a mark to measure yourself against – a checkpoint – as far as effort you've put in, versus the results you've achieved.

If your results aren't quite up to what you'd hoped for, then it's just a matter of taking on a few %age points more of the System we've set. This is also a very good way to trick an unwilling mind or body into doing what you want it to do.

Although this System is perfect for the busy person who wants to do as little as possible for maximum results, on its own, the nutritional section (what goes in your mouth), has had wonderful results, with many people achieving a great deal more than they thought they could, that is, without breaking into a sweat.

It would be negligent of me not to make you aware of the 100% System, for optimum results in the shortest amount of time (without cheating). This, of course, includes exercise (see Easy Exercise for Optimum Results section, p. 89). Try to keep in the front of your mind why you started on this body-shaping mission, and that too will help you keep right on track.

It's amazing to see what we see in our business. People from all walks of life all have the same desires and needs. Even when we lecture in large corporations, or when I meet with a group of housewives and mothers in one of their homes, wanting a better body shape is universal.

> Nothing spreads faster than wildfire except the news that someone who has been trying to lose weight for years has finally done it.

You will be amazed at how many people will look to you for support. This will also motivate and encourage you to maintain your new body shape.

Easy Exercise for *Every*BODY!

easy
exercise
for *every*BODY!

The
EASY
Body
Toning
System

Sequel to
bestseller
*Fat Free
Forever*

Dianne Barker

It's NOT just another exercise book. NOT another thing to start on Monday and give up on Tuesday! It's a life-changing system. Simple to read and easy to follow. It's truly the difference between looking good and looking great — *especially in a swimsuit!* This really is an easy 'how to book'.

Available at all good bookstores.

Chapter

13

Easy Exercise for Optimum Results

Exercise is something you simply cannot avoid if you want to fully achieve your body-shaping dreams. I can say it fast if it helps, or even whisper it, but you cannot ignore it. Exercise. It's a dirty word for some and a life-saving love for others. Although sitting is better than lying down, and standing is better than sitting, walking is much better than standing, but running is *not* better than walking. Confused? Read on.

Let's explore the reasons why anyone should bother with exercise if they are getting good results from the System without moving a muscle (which will happen).

Your body's ability to burn fat is very much dependent on the tone of your muscles. If they are strong and well-toned, you will be a far more efficient fat-munching machine. Now, I don't know about you, but if doing a little toning exercise will make the whole dieting thing a little easier, I for one am going to do it. By taking part in basic exercise, you can consume more foods that you enjoy, and at the same time turn even your everyday movements into efficient, fat-burning activities (mini workouts without you even realising that you're exercising).

> How you feel plays a large part in how you look.

Already, by following the System, you will notice that you are sleeping better, and that you have more energy. This is great, but there's more! I'm sure you'll agree, if something makes you feel and perform better than previously, it's going to be a pleasure to continue it and make it a routine part of your life. Exercise releases hormones called endorphins which are responsible for your body's feeling of well-being. If done correctly, the right type of exercise will help your body to increase its ability to produce these natural feel-good hormones, and therefore also increase your ability to cope with stress, worry, or just twentieth-century living!

> Use it or lose it!

Although *Fat Free Forever* is primarily a way of life that will ensure you have a better body shape, it also has another very positive side-effect – great health!

Unfortunately, most methods used to change body shapes have detrimental effects on the body's health, especially in the long term. This System does just the opposite. And, if you include an exercise programme in your new way of living, you are increasing the value of the body shaping 'insurance policy' you have just taken out by reading this book. It is literally a deposit, in your favour, in the body-shaping bank! Regular muscular stimulation is the only way, apart from good nutrition, to ensure maximum health, mobility and youthfulness as you age.

So, what does it take?

First of all, it's vital that you understand what exercise is before you can take part in it properly. You may have had quite extensive contact with various types of gym exercise, such as Step Reebok, aerobics, and circuit classes, or sports such as running, swimming, tennis or netball. You probably undertook this type of exercise with many good intentions, but more often than not, without the results which were promised or expected. Some of you may say it's your own fault for not being diligent enough, but it's usually true that it's just that you weren't doing the correct type of exercise, which would benefit a great body shape.

If you enjoy playing tennis, squash, netball or basketball, by all means, keep playing. But if you think it's all you need to get in shape, think again. Body shaping is definitely not a hit-and-miss thing. You can't just dip your hand into a big bag of activities and hope to achieve your goals by your good intentions, and a bit of sweat and luck to boot! If you consider body shaping a sport, then it may be easier to understand. Just as great jockeys like Darren Beadman don't play basketball to win the Melbourne Cup, and tennis players like Andre Agassi don't surf to win Wimbledon, it's important for you to understand that to achieve a better body shape, you have to train like a body shaper.

> Doing 50% of the right activity is a lot better than doing 100% of the wrong one. And believe me, there are right and wrong activities!

Have you ever seen a fat or podgy aerobics instructor? Every gym has at least one. Now why is it that these instructors, who take far more high-energy classes than you each week, are still overweight? Because they're usually eating wrong – overloading on carbs – so that even the several aerobics classes each week can't shift the fat. Can you see the equation here? High-impact aerobics classes just do not equal fat loss and better body shape.

And it's not just aerobics classes which shake the equation. Add to it running, jogging, and any other high energy activity. Why? Fat is slow-burning and is converted very slowly for use as a long-lasting, energy source.

> Fat must have oxygen to allow it to burn in the same way as a flame needs oxygen.

High-energy, high-impact activities demand a fast supply of fuel to keep them going. They also need a fuel that doesn't rely on oxygen: chances are you will be out of breath, so at these times the body will choose one of its fast energy providers, such as carbohydrates or glycogen energy. Therefore, little or no fat is burnt by doing these types of activities.

'Oh, no!', I hear you groan. Wasted years jumping around for nothing. Well, not entirely.

Your fitness level will have improved and you will have toned certain muscles to some degree, and you will have stimulated your metabolism to work a little faster, but as I mentioned earlier, we are now only interested in the 100% optimum most efficient ways to get in shape, so please, don't knock yourself out wasting any more time! Now you know why we called this chapter Easy Exercise.

Walking is probably the best fat-burning method known. It's also the easiest and least likely to cause injury, so use it. Cycling is also good. The trick is to keep a good pace (not breathing hard) for as long as possible. This will guarantee you are burning fat. If you measure your heart rate, you should use the following formula to determine if you are exercising at the best pace.

$$220 - \text{your age (a)} = b$$

$$60–70\% \text{ of } b = c$$

'c' is your maximum heart rate per minute for burning fat.

What's best about fat burning is that it can be done almost any time, anywhere, from a walk to and from work, or parking the car a little further from the office, or pushing your baby around the park. Even thirty minutes or more each day makes a big difference to your results (see Optimum Exercise Chart p. 99).

A brisk dawn or dusk stroll clears away the cobwebs and helps you think.

With fat burning taken care of, let's now deal with another issue. I'm not going to give you a pile of regular bum, tum and thigh exercises. They are probably why you've bought this book – because they haven't worked! It's not just the exercise you do, but it is, more importantly, how you do them.

I have absolutely no objection to any sport or current exercise programme you may already enjoy. Keep it up, if it's having the desired effect, that is increasing your fitness level, if your social or competitive needs are met, and if it is important to you. Basically, do it for pleasure.

> Weight or resistance training is the quickest proven method to change your body shape with the minimum amount of effort.

We call it body sculpting. Unfortunately, this area of exercise is very misunderstood. It is not unreasonable to assume that if you want to change your body shape you must work the body parts which are responsible for that shape, that is, bone, muscle and fat. Bone can't be changed, so that leaves us with muscle and fat. We have already addressed fat with good nutrition and walking, so that leaves only one thing to be shaped – muscle.

This is done most efficiently through direct stimulation, or *weight resistance*. One point to remember is that you *cannot* spot reduce. In other words, if you have a roll of fat on your tummy, doing 1000 sit ups, three times a day, is not going to get rid of it. The result of this type of overexercising will widen the stomach, not slim it down!

You will not be burning fat from the area you are training. The reason you are doing weight-resistance training is to firm your muscles and increase your body's ability as a whole to burn fat from wherever it sees fit. And, believe me, it's often not our choice of fat store – breasts, face, etc. – to go first. In fact, the general rule is, the bigger the fat store (bottom, hips, and thighs), the more likely it is that the body will leave it until last. So it's important to be patient and persistent – especially now you know why!

What kind of resistance training?

Most people know about lunges, leg raises, and squats. The stuff that Elle McPherson and Cindy Crawford get you doing in your living room. This area is another whole book! Exercise is a mind-blowing, complex issue, with numerous different types, styles and fads, and it's changing all the time.

This is not a bad thing, as everybody has different responses to different types of exercise. If I give you some vital points on resistance exercising, you can apply them to any routine or programme you may have been given in the past.

Even the old exercise video in your loungeroom can work wonders when you know what you're doing and why. No matter how average the programme you choose, or how little you know about training, if you follow *exactly* the following rules, *it will work*.

1   Find out exactly which area you are working when you exercise. If you are not 100% sure, ask someone who does. It's the most crucial part of training. When you know it, write it down.

2   When doing the exercise, concentrate completely on the area you are supposed to be working. Don't think about what's for dinner, or where you have to be next, or what the kids are doing.

We all know someone who has been training for years and still looks the same as when they started. Almost always this is due to lack of focus. They go through the motions without any thought to what is and isn't working. Don't waste your time – CONCENTRATE!

> Lack of concentration will render a perfectly good exercise useless.

3   If you cannot feel an exercise where you are supposed to, yet you are feeling it in an area you're not trying to work, simply adjust your position until you feel it where you should. Don't be afraid to shuffle your body into your correct position. Just because someone tells you you are supposed to do it like this or that, it's really irrelevant if you can't feel it, or if it's working a totally different area. Everyone is built differently, so make it work for you.

4   Effort is vital. Do not worry about how many times you are supposed to repeat an exercise; the rule is easy. Keep going until you can't go any more (at the same time, feeling it where you are supposed to), then stop and rest until you feel ready. Then do it again. Repeat this three or four times, or even up to five times, depending on how you feel.

Remember to monitor yourself carefully, so you don't overdo it in the beginning. Obviously, if you are unfit, you won't be able to do much and if you are fit, you'll be able to do a lot more. By following this, you will improve the muscle every time you train it, instead of stopping just about when the exercise starts to work for you.

5   Each time you do each exercise, do just a little more, building up slowly. It's a lot of fun and very inspirational to see how quickly you can improve.

6   Don't rush an exercise. Do them all slowly and deliberately, being aware of what is working through the up (bending or flexing) and the down (stretching or extending) of the movement.

> Remember when combining aerobic activity (walking, cycling, etc.) with weight-training, to do them in the correct order.

Because your body burns up energy, or glycogen, when it first starts training, it's important that you weight train first. Then, when you start your aerobic training, you will be instantly burning fat. If you do it the other way around, not only will you be lacking energy to weight train, but you have wasted the first half of your aerobic training, burning energy, and not fat! Simple but effective.

In summary, by applying the above principles, you will guarantee results. It is essential, however, that you apply all of them all the time. They are quite literally the key that makes the difference between those who shape up and those who don't.

The best thing for you to do is read my newest book, Easy Exercise for *Every*BODY! which explains in *easy* terms, how to achieve a beautifully toned physique. It really is the difference between what makes a good body and a *great* body – especially in a swimsuit! It's available in all good bookstores.

OPTIMUM EXERCISE CHART

Type of exercise	No. of days per week	Duration per day
Fat Burning		
Walking or Cycling	3–5 days	30–60 minutes
Muscle Tone		
Weights	3–5 days	30–60 minutes

This chart has been designed as a simple guide with which you can assess your own programme. Do what-ever you can fit into your schedule, and try to make improvements over time as you become more comfortable with the exercise. Don't eat before exercising, and try to eat 30 minutes after you've finished.

Chapter 14

Food Flavourings

If oil didn't exist, you wouldn't be able to use it. The same goes for cream, butter, margarine and mayonnaise. Life may be completely boring without this wonderful variety of fattening flavours, but they *are* fattening flavours, and should be put into a separate category, away from the flavours you will use in everyday life.

Your supermarket shelves are full of wonderful fattening-flavour alternatives. Any brands I've listed throughout the No-Fat Recipes section are there because I've found them to be the lowest in fat. You may find other flavours and other brands; by all means use them. You know what the boundaries are, so just work within them.

The main essentials are Teflon (or similar non-stick) cookware. Without these, it's too tempting to use a little oil or spray so the food doesn't stick. The other important skill you will learn, besides weeding out the flavours with oil and the flavours without, will be timing your cooking. Cooking without any oil or cooking spray can be tricky at first. Once you get used to it, it's pretty easy. You have to be careful not to dry food out, you will also become quite skilled at splashing in a little water, just to help food go golden, but not letting it go soggy. It's a fine line, but time and experimenting and patience will get you through this learning stage.

I want to encourage you to be as creative as possible when it comes to the flavour and colour of the foods you eat. This is a major factor in keeping you on the System.

> Where there's variety, there's no boredom!
> Anyway, whoever said fat is flavour?

There are very few recipes that I haven't been able to completely copy in taste, texture and looks. There are some that I simply cannot, but to help you overcome the whole taste issue, if that's important to you, simply say to yourself, 'Oil doesn't exist', and then prepare and cook accordingly. You must realise that if it's not exactly the same as it is with olive oil, then that's purely a choice issue only you can make.

> Don't let the tastebuds on your tongue,
> determine the big bumps on your bum!

FOOD FLAVOURINGS CHART

Remember, no fat, oil, butter, margarine, cream, and very limited sugar.

salt
pepper
all herbs (fresh/dry)
all spices
mustard (oil-free)
soy sauce
teriyaki sauce
Worcestershire sauce
chilli and ginger sauces
most stock flavourings

garlic
oyster sauce
some tinned soups
French onion soup mix
tomato paste
vinegar (any kind)
oil-free salad dressings
honey
low-joule dessert toppings
small amounts of artificial
sweeteners

Chapter 15

Let's Go Shopping

Most people are careful shoppers when it comes to keeping within their financial budget, but don't have a clue about how to keep within a body shaping budget! 90% of processed foods can be classified unhealthy, as they're very high in fat, so they're automatically eliminated from the shopping list, to be replaced by fresh, natural foods.

Again, any brand names I've mentioned are because at the time of writing, they were the lowest in fat, best in taste and most convenient to buy. You know your perimeters, so develop a list by integrating mine with your own personal tastes.

Remember, anything marked 'light' or 'low' can be light and/or low in colour, texture, taste, cholesterol and everything else except fat! Some foods marked 'low fat' are required by law to be only 25% less than the regular food. So please be careful.

SHOPPING LIST

> Everything should be available in your
> supermarket, or I've listed where else to look.
> Remember to watch the fat content of everything!

UHT skim milk
eggs
Danone Diet Lite flavoured yoghurts
Life-Body Shaping Food/LITE Body Shaping Milk
    99% fat free (see p. 237)
Trim-Life Amino low cal soft drinks
Vita Brits, Weetbix or similar low fat, high-fibre cereal
cracked black pepper
rock salt
Maggi Seasoning sauce
Ayam brand seasoning powders (Asian grocery stores)
Continental French Onion Soup mix
Continental Beef, Chicken and Vegetable Stock powders
                (no added msg)
oyster sauce
teriyaki sauce
Goodness brand muesli
100% fruit jams (Monbulk or Berri) – no sugar
or artificial sweeteners added
Cottee's Low Joule Chocolate Sauce
Ovaltine (not Ovaltine Light)
a selection of starchy carbohydrates
fresh lean meat
fresh fruit and vegetables
herbs (fresh or dry)
flavourings listed in Food Flavourings (see p. 102)

fat free forever!
The Cook Book
your favourite recipes from around the globe

fat free
forever!

The

Cook Book

your favourite recipes from around the globe

by Dianne Barker

New Release 1999

Due to the overwhelming and ongoing success of **Fat Free Forever!** Dianne is writing **Fat Free Forever, The Cook Book** which will contain 100 new and exciting fat free recipes from around the globe.

The Cook Book is the first in Dianne's series of excellent fat free cook books which will be released over the next few years. This particular release will focus on favourite recipes from around the globe. Dianne transforms the most popular dishes into delicious culinary masterpieces – fat free!

Fat Free Forever — THE COOK BOOK will be available in 1999.

Chapter 16

No-Fat Recipes

These No-Fat Recipes evolved from a long process of elimination. As I've said, it's important that you increase the amount of variety in your diet, as you will then be less likely to think about food as a major issue. To help you, I've included plenty of variety but by all means, add some flavours of your own. Never say never when it comes to transforming fat to fat free. Just put your mind and tastebuds to the test, and give it a go.

You know by now that my theory is, 'If you can see the fat it's too much'. As there are enough natural fats in foods, I have designed recipes and cooking methods around utilising this minimal amount of unseen fat.

What is unique about this section of the book, is its coding system, which has been designed to make life easier for you. You can quickly turn to any recipe and not have to work out if it's protein, carbs, or the time of day it should be eaten. When you start cooking, you will soon become aware of these without even looking.

NO-FAT RECIPES CODING SYSTEM

Each recipe has three faces at the top of the page.

☺ **eat it and enjoy**

☻ **eat it if you must**
(something else would be better)

☹ **don't eat it!**

B, **D** and **L** are written beneath the faces, and they indicate when you can eat each recipe.

B   Breakfast

L   Lunch

D   Dinner

Di's Favourites

Farmhouse Muesli

Big Breakfast

Penne with Tomatoes and Basil

Unfried Chicken Strips

Springtime Stir Fry

B   L   D

Farmhouse Muesli

Large Starchy Carbohydrate/
Small Fibrous Carbohydrate
20 minutes to make
Serves 2 adults

Ingredients

½ cup dried prunes
½ cup dried apricots
2 cups hot water
2 cups quick cooking oats
4 tablespoons low-fat (97–8% fat free) muesli
2–3 cups skim milk

Method

1 Heat prunes and apricots in hot water in the microwave for 10–20 minutes, depending on what type of microwave you have, and let sit until plump.

2 Into a medium Teflon saucepan, place oats, muesli and milk. Stir thoroughly. If possible, allow to soak cold for 10–15 minutes.

3 Cook on a low to medium heat for approximately 10 min-
utes, ensuring a creamy texture. Add a little more milk if necessary. Make sure the mixture isn't gluggy.

4 Serve piping hot with warm prunes, apricots and honey, and a little milk if desired.

Big Breakfast

B L D

Large Protein/Medium Carbohydrate (optional)
20 minutes to make
Serves 2 adults

Ingredients

- 4 slices 98% fat-free smoked ham
- 1 heaped teaspoon Continental Chicken Stock powder *or* 1 Continental Chicken Stock cube
- ½ cup water
- 2 large ripe tomatoes
- handful fresh champignons
- your choice of eggs

Method

1 Begin cooking ham in half the chicken stock and half the water in a small Teflon frypan. Cover with a lid after one side has browned. Add a little extra water if necessary.

2 In a separate frypan, cook the tomatoes in chunks, along with the champignons and the remaining chicken stock and water.

3 Cook your choice of eggs as per the recipes in the Eggs section (pp. 119–24).

4 Serve immediately with toast (no butter) and some Chipped Potato Grits (p. 198). (No toast and no potatoes if you are eating this meal for dinner.)

Penne with Tomatoes and Basil

B L D

Large Carbohydrate/Small Protein
20 minutes to make
Serves at least 4 adults

Ingredients

3 cups water
1 small packet penne pasta
2 small tins whole peeled tomatoes (without oil and, if
   possible, without sugar)
2 teaspoons fresh or 1 teaspoon dried basil
$1/2$ teaspoon rock salt
$1/2$ teaspoon cracked black pepper
$1/4$ cup chopped spring onions

Method

1 In a large saucepan, boil the water, and add the penne. Add more water if necessary. Cook only until soft. It takes approximately 15–20 minutes.
2 Place the rest of the ingredients in a medium-sized Teflon saucepan. Stir well and simmer on low–medium heat for 30 minutes, or until liquid is fairly reduced.
3 Drain and wash the pasta well and place it into a large container for serving.
4 Pour the sauce over the pasta and mix well.
5 Serve with a fresh side salad.

Unfried Chicken Strips

B L D

Large Protein
15 minutes to make
Serves 4 adults

Ingredients

3 double chicken breast fillets (skinless and boneless)
1¹/₂ cups self-raising flour
³/₄ cup Masterfood's Cajun spices
cracked black pepper and rock salt to taste
4 eggs (1 yolk only)
¹/₃ cup teriyaki sauce

Method

1 Wash chicken and remove any traces of fat. Cut each half breast into 4 strips.
2 Empty the flour, spices, salt and pepper onto greaseproof paper and mix thoroughly.
3 In a separate bowl, whisk the eggs with the sauce.
4 Heat a large Teflon frypan on high until the pan is really hot.
5 Roll each chicken strip in the flour mixture, then dip in the egg mixture, then into the flour mixture again.
6 Place strips straight into the hot pan. Cover with a lid.
7 After 5–7 minutes, turn the strips over (they should look greyish). Replace the lid and cook a further 3–4 minutes.
8 Remove lid and splash a little water over chicken so it starts to look golden. Replace lid. It's important that there are no puddles of water in the pan. Turn and splash until the golden colour comes through most of each strip.
9 Cook for a further 2 minutes. Remove.

This frying/steaming combination creates a great taste while keeping the chicken moist and succulent.

Springtime Stir Fry

B   L   D

Medium Fibrous Carbohydrate/Small Protein
20 minutes to make
Serves 4 adults

Ingredients

2 cups fresh green beans
1 cup fresh snow peas
1 cup shredded butternut pumpkin
1 cup shredded cabbage
$^1/_2$ cup bean sprouts
1 teaspoon Continental French Onion Soup mix
1 teaspoon Masterfood's Cajun spices
rock salt and cracked black pepper to taste
$^1/_2$ cup white wine

Method

1 Preheat a large Teflon frypan while preparing vegetables.
2 Combine all the ingredients, place in frypan
and place a lid on top.
3 After 10 minutes or so, stir and replace the lid.
4 Remove when vegies are soft enough for you.
5 Serve hot on their own, or with some grilled chicken strips.

Protein Shakes

Strawberry Smoothie

Passionfruit Malt Shake

Crushed Fruit Splice

Iced Coffee Shake

Swiss Chocolate Shake

B   L   D

Strawberry Smoothie

Large Protein
2 minutes to make
Serves 1 adult

Ingredients

2 cups skim milk
3 heaped dessertspoons Life-Body Shaping Food
handful fresh strawberries
200 gram Danone Diet Lite Strawberry Yoghurt

Method

1 Using a container which will hold up to 3 cups of liquid, pour in the milk. *(Make <u>sure</u> the milk is added first!)*
2 Add the other ingredients.
3 Blend well.
4 Drink straightaway while chilled, or take with you in a flask to drink throughout the day.

Passionfruit Malt Shake

Large Protein
2 minutes to make
Serves 1 adult

Ingredients

2 cups skim milk
3 heaped dessertspoons Life-Body Shaping Food
200 gram Danone Diet Lite Passionfruit Yoghurt
pulp of 1 small, fresh passionfruit (if in season)
1 heaped teaspoon malt
3 dessertspoons no-fat, low-sugar natural yoghurt

Method

1 Using a container which will hold up to 3 cups of liquid, pour in the milk. *(Make <u>sure</u> the milk is added first!)*
2 Add the other ingredients.
3 Blend well.
4 Drink straightaway while chilled, or take with you in a flask to drink throughout the day.

B   L   D

Crushed Fruit Splice

Large Protein
Takes 2 minutes to make
Serves 1 adult

Ingredients

2 cups skim milk
2 cups 100% apple juice (no added sugar)
3 dessertspoons low-fat, no-sugar natural yoghurt
3 heaped dessertspoons Life-Body Shaping Food
½ cup fresh fruit, roughly chopped (no banana)
½ cup ice

Method

1 Using a large container that can hold 3 cups, pour in the milk. *(Make <u>sure</u> the milk is added first!)*
2 Add the juice and yoghurt.
3 Now add other ingredients.
4 Blend well.
5 Serve with a garnish of fresh strawberries.

B L D

Iced Coffee Shake

Large Protein
2 minutes to make
Serves 1 adult

Ingredients

2 cups skim milk
3 heaped dessertspoons Life-Body Shaping Food
½ cup espresso coffee
1 teaspoon Splendid or Equal (to taste)

Method

1 Using a container that can hold 3 cups, pour in the milk. *(Make sure the milk is added first!)*
2 Add the other ingredients.
3 Blend well.
4 Drink while chilled, or take with you in a flask to drink throughout the day.

B L D

Swiss Chocolate Shake

Large Protein
2 minutes to make
Serves 1 adult

Ingredients

2 cups skim milk
3 heaped dessertspoons Life-Body Shaping Food
3 dessertspoons Cottee's Low Joule Chocolate Sauce

Method

1 Using a container which will hold up to 3 cups of liquid, pour in the milk. *(Make <u>sure</u> the milk is added first!)*
2 Add the other ingredients.
3 Blend well.
4 Drink while chilled, or take with you in a flask to drink throughout the day.

Eggs

Gourmet Scrambled Eggs

French Toast

Savoury Omelette

Toad in the Hole

Curried Egg and Lettuce Sandwiches

Gourmet Scrambled Eggs

B   L   D

Large Protein/Small Carbohydrate (optional)
10 minutes to make
Serves 2 adults

Ingredients

10 large eggs
2 teaspoons freshly chopped parsley
½ cup skim milk
rock salt and cracked black pepper to taste
4 pieces thickly sliced bread for toasting
    (only if it's breakfast or lunch)
Maggi Seasoning sauce

Method

1 Remove 3 out of 5 yolks.
2 Heat a medium Teflon frypan and add all the ingredients.
  Stir occasionally.
3 When the eggs are nearly done, remove from the heat,
  stirring from the base of the pan.
4 Serve immediately on hot, unbuttered toast (no toast if eating for dinner) with a sprinkle of Maggi Seasoning.

Note If you accidentally cook the eggs right through, add
whole egg and mix quickly through the scrambled eggs. This
should make them nice and creamy again.

French Toast

Medium Protein/Medium Carbohydrate
5 minutes to make
Serves 2 adults

Ingredients

1 tank loaf white bread
4 large eggs
2 tablespoons skim milk
rock salt and cracked black pepper to taste
1 tomato *or* maple syrup

Method

1 Slice 4 pieces of bread approximately 2 cm thick.
2 In a medium bowl, whisk the eggs, milk, salt and pepper.
3 Briefly soak each slice of bread in the egg mixture.
4 Heat a large Teflon frypan. Place the soaked bread in pan.
5 When browned, turn the bread over.
6 When both sides are browned, serve with grilled tomatoes or, if you've been good, a small dash of maple syrup!

B L D

Savoury Omelette

Large Protein
10 minutes to make
Serves 1 adult

Ingredients

4 large eggs (2 yolks only)
2 teaspoons parsley, freshly chopped
1 teaspoon Continental French Onion Soup mix
1 small tomato, chopped
$^1/_2$ small onion, chopped
$^1/_2$ cup spring onions, chopped
crunchy vegetables, freshly chopped
rock salt and cracked black pepper to taste

Method

1 Beat eggs well in a medium mixing bowl.
2 Add remaining ingredients.
3 Heat a medium Teflon frypan and add the mixture.
4 When the base is cooked and coming away from the sides of the pan, remove the omelette from the stove and place under a preheated griller until the mixture is well cooked and lightly browned on top.
5 Remove the omelette carefully by folding one half on top of the other, then sliding it onto a warmed plate.
6 Serve with a crunchy garden salad.

B   L   D

Toad in the Hole

Medium Protein/Medium Carbohydrate
15 minutes to make
Serves 1 adult

Ingredients

3 large eggs
1 teaspoon parsley, freshly chopped
rock salt and cracked black pepper to taste
2 thick slices white or wholemeal bread
1 ripe tomato
Maggi Seasoning sauce

Method

1 In a small mixing bowl, beat 1 egg and add the parsley, salt and pepper.
2 Cut out a small square in the middle of each slice of bread – the size of an egg yolk.
3 Dip the bread in the egg mixture.
4 Heat a large Teflon frypan and add the bread.
5 Crack 1 egg into the middle of each slice of bread.
6 Place a lid on the pan, and as soon as the bottom of the bread is browned, carefully turn over.
7 Depending on whether you like your eggs runny or hard, remove accordingly.
8 Serve hot with grilled tomatoes, fresh parsley and a sprinkle of Maggi Seasoning sauce.

Curried Egg and Lettuce Sandwiches   B   L   D

Medium Protein/Medium Carbohydrate
15 minutes to make
Serves 2 adults

Ingredients

3 large eggs
8 thick slices white *or* wholemeal bread
1 teaspoon curry powder
2 teaspoons tomato sauce
1 tablespoon skim milk (plus a little extra if required)
1 teaspoon parsley, freshly chopped
rock salt and cracked black pepper to taste

Method

1 In a small saucepan, hard boil the eggs.
2 Remove after cooked (approximately 10 minutes), and peel shell under cold water.
3 In a small mixing bowl, place the eggs and other ingredients.
4 Mix thoroughly until nice and creamy, adding extra milk if necessary.
5 Chop the lettuce finely.
6 Spoon egg mixture onto bread and sprinkle lettuce on top.
7 Cut sandwiches into fingers and serve with a garnish of fresh parsley.

Fish

Creamy Tuna Mornay

Grilled Fish with Lemon and Herbs

Fijian Baked Fish with Tomato Seasoning

Red Salmon Salad

Tuna Chowder

Creamy Tuna Mornay

B L D

Large Protein/Medium Carbohydrate (optional)
15 minutes to make
Serves 4 adults

Ingredients

4 eggs
1½ cups white rice
2 cups water
1 Continental Cheese Sauce packet mix
1 Lawry's Stroganoff Sauce packet mix
2 cups skim milk
425 gram tin of tuna in brine or springwater
rock salt and cracked black pepper to taste
1 lemon

Method

1 Hard boil eggs in small saucepan.
2 Boil rice in medium saucepan in water. Be careful not to overcook. Add more water if necessary.
3 Place cheese and stroganoff sauce mixes in a medium Teflon saucepan with the milk. Whisk well and keep stirring over a medium heat.
4 Drain the tuna. When the sauce is thickened, add tuna to the sauce. Add extra milk or brine if necessary to ensure mixture doesn't become gluggy.
5 Chop eggs into chunks and add to the tuna and sauce, along with salt and pepper.
6 Serve hot on a bed rice with a slice of lemon. (No rice if you eat this dish in the evening.)

Grilled Fish with Lemon and Herbs

B L D

Large Protein/Small Fibrous Carbohydrate
10 minutes to make
Serves 4 adults

Ingredients

4 large fillets of fresh, fleshy white fish (trevally, snapper, roughie)
4 squares of foil big enough to envelop fish fillets
2 teaspoons mixed herbs
2 lemons
cracked black pepper and rock salt to taste

Method

1 Wash fish and place individually in the centre of each piece of foil.
2 Add herbs, a good squeeze of lemon, a generous amount of salt and pepper.
3 Make a little package of the foil so no lemon juice escapes.
4 Close the packages like a pastie with the seam on top.
5 Place on a tray and, under a medium–high heat, grill for approximately 7 minutes.
6 Open packages and return to grill for another few minutes until the fish starts to brown.
7 Serve with a wedge of lemon and fresh garden salad.

Fijian Baked Fish with Tomato Seasoning

Medium Protein
45 minutes to make
Serves 4 adults

Ingredients

1 deep-sea bream (gutted and scaled)
1 large tomato
1 large onion
1 lemon
2 spring onion stalks
pinch of rock salt

Method

1 Wash the fish thoroughly and place on a large sheet of foil (big enough to fold over).
2 Slice the tomato, onion and lemon in circles.
3 Chop the spring onions (not too finely).
4 Spread the ingredients on top of the fish. Add a pinch of salt.
5 Wrap foil over the fish and bake for 30 minutes at 180°C (350°F).
6 Serve with your favourite non-starch salad.

B   L   D

Red Salmon Salad

Large Protein/Medium Carbohydrate (optional)
10 minutes to make
Serves 4 adults

Ingredients

425 gram tin of red salmon
1 small onion, finely chopped
1 tablespoon parsley, freshly chopped
2 medium carrots, roughly chopped
2 large celery stalks, roughly chopped
$\frac{1}{2}$ a red or green (or both) capsicum, roughly chopped
$\frac{1}{4}$ cup lemon juice
Kraft Oil Free French or Italian salad dressing
rock salt or cracked black pepper to taste

Method

1 Place all ingredients in a large mixing bowl and mix thoroughly.
2 Serve either hot or cold over white rice or with a dry-baked jacket potato (only if you're eating this for lunch). You can serve it with a green salad for early dinner.

Tuna Chowder

B L D

Medium Protein/Small Starchy/Small Fibrous Carbohydrate
40 minutes to make
Serves at least 4 adults

Ingredients

2 large tins of tuna in brine or spring water
(drain one tin only)
2 celery stalks, diced
1 medium onion, diced
1 large potato, diced (leave the skin on)
8 mushrooms, sliced
½ teaspoon dill
2 tablespoons Continental Chicken Stock powder
4 cups water
1 small tin evaporated skim milk
rock salt and cracked black pepper to taste
cornflour (if needed)

Method

1 In a large saucepan, combine all the ingredients.
2 Bring to the boil, then reduce the heat. Put a lid on the saucepan and simmer for approximately 30 minutes, stirring occasionally.
3 If you wish to thicken the chowder, carefully add cornflour after you've blended it with a little water in a separate bowl.
4 If you are eating this for lunch, a great idea is to empty out some large, heavy, white-bread rolls, and pour in the chowder. Saves on bowls, and it's a great entertaining idea.

Chicken

Honey Chicken

Chicken Schnitzel with Lemon Sauce

Lemon Herb Chicken

Chicken in Homemade Barbecue Sauce

Chicken Cordon Bleu

Honey Chicken

B L D

Large Protein/Medium Carbohydrate (optional)
20 minutes to make
Serves at least 4 adults

Ingredients

2 cups quick brown rice
6 large chicken breast fillets (skinless and boneless)
1 large onion
1 teaspoon Continental Chicken Stock powder
1 tablespoon parsley, freshly chopped
4 tablespoons honey
1 cup cold water

Method

1 Begin cooking rice in a large saucepan of boiling water, stirring occasionally, adding more water if necessary.
2 Chop the chicken into large, bite-sized pieces.
3 In a large Teflon frypan, cook the chicken, onion, stock, parsley, honey and water on medium-high temperature until chicken is brown.
4 Reduce temperature and remove lid. Cook until sauce thickens slightly (a hot toffee-like consistency).
5 Turn stove off. Add a little water if sauce is too thick, and cover pan with lid.
6 Remove rice from heat and wash thoroughly using a colander.
7 Serve honey chicken on rice with a side serve of lightly steamed carrots, corn and broccoli. (No rice if you're eating this meal in the evening.)

Chicken Schnitzel with Lemon Sauce   B L D

Large Protein/Small Fibrous Carbohydrate
25 minutes to make
Serves 4 adults

Ingredients

4 large chicken breast fillets (skinless and boneless)
2 cups breadcrumbs
2 teaspoons cracked black pepper and rock salt to taste
2 cups cornflour
2 teaspoons sweet paprika
2 eggs
2 tablespoons Gravox Seasoned Chicken Gravy mix
juice of 1 lemon
1 cup water

Method

1 Wash chicken and remove any traces of fat.
2 Prepare 2 sheets of greaseproof paper.
3 Place breadcrumbs with salt mixed in well on one sheet, and cornflour, pepper and paprika, mixed well, on the other sheet.
4 In a small bowl, beat eggs well.
5 Roll the chicken in the cornflour, then dip in the beaten egg, then roll in the breadcrumbs.
6 Place chicken in a preheated Teflon frypan. When one side is slightly brown, turn chicken and place a lid on the pan.
7 Check carefully that the chicken has cooked through and that it has browned. Remove from the heat.
8 Add Gravox, lemon juice and water (a little at a time), to a separate Teflon saucepan. Stir until thick. Pour over the chicken schnitzel.
9 Serve with crunchy salad vegetables. Garnish with a slice of lemon.

Lemon Herb Chicken

B   L   D

Large Protein/Small Fibrous Carbohydrate
15 minutes to make
Serves 4 adults

Ingredients

4 large chicken breast fillets (skinless and boneless)
2 teaspoons dried mixed herbs
1 teaspoon Continental French Onion Soup mix
2 lemons
4 tablespoons water
cracked black pepper and rock salt to taste

Method

1 Wash chicken and leave it in whole fillets.
2 Place in medium-sized Teflon frypan.
3 Add herbs, the juice of 1½ lemons, French Onion Soup mix, water, pepper and salt.
4 Begin to cook at a medium–high temperature.
5 Place a lid on the saucepan after one side of chicken has been seared and turned over. Reduce heat slightly.
6 After a few minutes the chicken will be cooked (be careful not to overcook and dry out). Add a little more lemon if necessary.
7 Serve with a wedge of lemon and a fresh garden salad.

B   L   D

Chicken in Homemade Barbecue Sauce

Large Protein/Medium Fibrous/
Starchy Carbohydrate (optional)
60 minutes to make
Serves 4–6 adults

Ingredients

6 half chicken breast fillets
powdered black pepper
1 dessertspoon Continental Chicken Stock powder
1 medium onion, finely chopped
¼ cup cold water
5 tablespoons white wine
5 tablespoons soy sauce
1 heaped tablespoon tomato purée
1 heaped teaspoon mustard powder
1 teaspoon crushed garlic

Method

1 Preheat oven to 200°C (400°F).
2 Wash and dry fillets very well and slice in half. Rub each piece all over with pepper and some of the stock.
3 Place chicken into a shallow roasting pan, tucking the onion among the pieces. Sprinkle them with the remaining stock and a few drops of water.
4 Place the pan on the highest oven shelf and cook for 30 minutes.
5 Whisk sauce ingredients until blended, then pour over the chicken. Cook for a further 25 minutes, basting frequently.
7 Serve hot with brown rice and a crisp garden salad. (No rice if eating this meal for dinner.)

Chicken Cordon Bleu

B L D

Large Protein/Small Fibrous Carbohydrate
25 minutes to make
Serves 4 adults

Ingredients

4 large chicken breast fillets (skinless and boneless)
2 large slices 98% fat-free smoked ham (available from your local Deli)
2 slices reduced-fat cheese
8 toothpicks
1 teaspoon Continental French Onion Soup mix
$1/2$ cup water
cracked black pepper and rock salt to taste

Method

1 Wash chicken and remove any traces of fat.
2 Slice chicken in half as you would a bread roll, not quite all the way through.
3 Poke in half a slice of ham and half a slice of cheese.
4 Stitch up along each side with two toothpicks per chicken breast.
5 Heat a large Teflon frypan and add the French Onion Soup mix and water.
6 When sauce is mixed and heated, add the chicken fillets. Keep temperature fairly high until one side is slightly browned.
7 Turn chicken over, place lid on frypan and reduce heat to low–medium. Add a little more water if necessary.
8 Serve with steamed winter vegetables and a sprinkle of parsley. (Don't forget – no starchy carbs if you eat this meal in the evening!)

Veal

Vienna Schnitzel

Veal Stroganoff

Italian Veal Casserole

Cajun Veal Kebabs

Veal and Broccoli in Creamy Cheese Sauce

Vienna Schnitzel

B L D

Large Protein/Medium Fibrous Carbohydrate (optional)
30 minutes to make
Serves 4 adults

Ingredients

1 cup breadcrumbs
rock salt and cracked black pepper to taste
1 cup cornflour
sweet paprika
2 eggs
2 tablespoons lemon juice
6 large, very lean veal schnitzel fillets
1 small tube of anchovy paste (optional)
Gravox Low Joule Beef Gravy (optional)
2 tablespoons lemon juice (optional)

Method

1 Prepare 2 sheets of greaseproof paper.
2 Place breadcrumbs with salt mixed in well on one sheet of greaseproof paper, and cornflour, pepper and paprika mixed well on the other.
3 In a small bowl, beat eggs with the lemon juice.
4 Coat the meat in anchovy sauce if using it. Roll meat in the cornflour. Dip it in the egg, then roll in the breadcrumbs.
5 Place the veal in a large, preheated Teflon frypan.
6 When one side of the meat has browned slightly, turn it over and place a lid on the pan.
7 It will cook quickly, so be careful not to overcook. When browned and cooked through, remove from the heat.
8 Serve with slightly steamed vegetables and a slice of lemon. If desired, also serve Gravox Low Joule Beef Gravy with the lemon juice.

B L D

Veal Stroganoff

Large Protein/Medium Starchy Carbohydrate (optional)
20 minutes to make
Serves 4 adults

Ingredients

1 kilo very lean veal, finely diced
1 dessertspoon Continental Chicken Stock powder
1/2 cup water
1 cup champignons
2 packets Lawry's Stroganoff mix
1 1/2–2 cups skim milk
rock salt and cracked black pepper to taste

Method

1 Lightly brown the veal in the stock and water in a medium–large Teflon frypan. Chop and add the champignons.
2 In a small Teflon saucepan, mix the stroganoff sauce with milk until thickened.
3 Pour the sauce into the frypan. Reduce the sauce if necessary.
4 When the meat and sauce have browned slightly, remove from heat.
5 Serve hot over brown and wild rice. (No rice if you eat this dish in the evening.)

Italian Veal Casserole

B L D

Large Protein/Medium Fibrous Carbohydrate (optional)
40 minutes to make
Serves 4 adults

Ingredients

1 medium onion, roughly chopped
1 teaspoon Continental Chicken Stock powder
1 kilo very lean veal, finely diced
½ cup water
275 mL white wine
350 grams tomatoes, peeled and chopped
1 tablespoon tomato paste
rock salt and cracked black pepper to taste
2 cloves chopped garlic, parsley and lemon rind for garnish

Method

1 In a large Teflon frypan, cook the onion and garlic in the chicken stock and water until golden (about 10 minutes).
2 Add the veal and brown slightly on both sides.
3 Pour in wine and let it bubble and reduce a little before adding tomatoes, tomato paste, and salt and pepper.
4 Cover the pan and allow meat to cook slowly for 20 minutes. Remove the lid and let the casserole cook gently for another 10 minutes or until the sauce has reduced.
5 Garnish with chopped garlic, parsley and lemon rind and serve with lightly steamed vegetables. (No starchy carbohydrates if you eat this meal in the evening).

B   L   D

Cajun Veal Kebabs

Large Protein/Medium Starchy Carbohydrate (optional)
30 minutes to make
Serves 4 adults

Ingredients

750 grams of lean, bite-sized cubes of veal
1 cup S & W Cajun Sauce
2 large onions
2 large capsicums, red and green
1 small tin unsweetened pineapple (fresh if available)
1 lemon
rock salt and cracked black pepper to taste
12 kebab skewers

Method

1 Marinade the veal in the Cajun sauce for half a day if possible, or for at least one hour.
2 Chop the onion and capsicums into large, bite-sized pieces.
3 Alternatively skewer the veal, onion, pineapple, capsicum, until skewer is full.
4 Using the same or a little extra Cajun sauce, continue to marinade the kebabs for approximately 20 minutes.
5 If you have the facilities, they are best barbecued. If not, cook in a very hot Teflon frypan or grill. Ensure that you don't over or undercook.
6 Serve immediately over white and wild rice with a slice of lemon. (Serve without rice if you are eating this dish in the evening.)

Veal and Broccoli in Creamy Cheese Sauce

B   L   D

Medium Protein/Small Fibrous Carbohydrate/ Medium Starchy Carbohydrate (optional)
20 minutes to make
Serves 4 adults

Ingredients

1 kilo very lean veal, finely diced
1 dessertspoon Continental Chicken Stock powder
rock salt and cracked black pepper to taste
1 medium onion, chopped
2 packets Continental Cheese Sauce mix
1 cup skim milk
¼ cup white wine
1 large head of broccoli chopped into small, bite-sized pieces
½ cup spring onions, finely chopped

Method

1 In a large Teflon frypan with lid on, lightly brown the veal in the stock, salt and pepper, white wine, spring onions and onion.
2 In a separate bowl, mix the cheese sauce and milk.
3 When veal is nearly cooked, add the broccoli and simmer for 5 minutes on a low heat with the lid on.
4 Add the cheese sauce mixture and stir well.
5 Allow to simmer for a further 5 minutes and let the cheese sauce go slightly brown.
6 Serve nice and hot over jasmine rice. (No rice if you eat this dish in the evening.)

Beef

Satay Beef with Fresh Garden Greens

Fillet Steak in Oyster Sauce

Fillet Steak with Dijon Mustard, Garlic and Pepper

Beef Curry with Whole Spices

Meatloaf with Barbecue Sauce

Satay Beef with Fresh Garden Greens   B L D

Large Protein/Small Fibrous Carbohydrate/
Small Starchy Carbohydrate (optional)
20 minutes to make
Serves 4 adults

Ingredients

6 fillet steaks, 1 inch thick
sweet paprika
4 tablespoons Ayam Satay Seasoning powder
1 teaspoon rock salt
1 dessertspoon Continental Beef Stock powder
1 small onion, chopped
1 large head of broccoli, chopped into small, bite-sized pieces
1 tablespoon Low Joule Beef Gravox
1 cup water

Method

1 Trim the steak of all fat and cut into thin, small strips.
2 Mix the paprika and satay seasoning with the salt.
3 Rub the mixture into the meat thoroughly and leave to marinade for as long as possible.
4 Using a large Teflon frypan on a high heat place the steak in the pan with the stock, half a cup of water and the onions.
5 When the steak is nearly cooked, add the broccoli.
6 Mix the Gravox with half a cup of water in a separate bowl.
7 When broccoli has just softened, pour in Gravox mixture.
8 Allow to simmer on a low heat for 5 minutes. Add a little more water if necessary.
9 Serve with a crunchy garden salad and a small serve of rice. Definitely no rice if you eat this meal in the evening.

Fillet Steak in Oyster Sauce

B L D

Large Protein/Small Fibrous Carbohydrate/ Small Starchy Carbohydrate (optional)
25 minutes to make
Serves 4 adults

Ingredients

6 fillet steaks, 1 inch thick
1 onion, thinly sliced
1 teaspoon Continental Beef Stock powder
½ cup water
1 cup bamboo shoots
cracked black pepper
4 tablespoons oyster sauce
1 dessertspoon soy sauce
2 cups whole baby green beans

Method

1 Remove all fat from steak and cut into thin, bite-sized strips.
2 In a large Teflon frypan, cook the steak with the onion, stock, water and pepper.
3 Just before steak is cooked, add the oyster sauce, bamboo shoots, beans and soy sauce.
4 Simmer for 5 minutes on a low heat, being very careful not to overcook.
5 When sauce has reduced slightly, place lid on pan and turn off heat.
6 Serve on a bed of jasmine rice with lightly steamed Chinese vegetables. (No rice if you eat this dish in the evening.)

B L D

Fillet Steak with Dijon Mustard, Garlic and Pepper

Large Protein/Small Fibrous Carbohydrate
25 minutes to make
Serves 4 adults

Ingredients

4 fillet steaks, 1½ inches thick
2 tablespoons Dijon seed mustard (no oil)
1 teaspoon crushed garlic
2 teaspoons cracked black pepper
½ teaspoon rock salt
½ cup Fountain Thick Teriyaki Sauce
½ cup water

Method

1 Remove all fat from steak and place into a shallow dish to marinade with all of the other ingredients except the water.
2 In a medium, preheated Teflon frypan, sear the steak both sides then add the rest of the marinade.
3 Reduce the heat and cook until steak is done to taste.
4 Add water a little at a time only if necessary. If necessary, add a little more teriyaki sauce.
5 Serve with thinly-sliced carrots and steamed green vegetables.

Beef Curry with Whole Spices

B   L   D

Large Protein/Medium Starchy Carbohydrate (optional)
30 minutes to make (plus 2 hours simmering time)
Serves 4 adults

Ingredients

2 teaspoons coriander seeds, crushed
1 teaspoon cumin seeds, crushed
1 tablespoon turmeric
700 grams fillet steak, all fat removed, cut into strips
2 large onions, sliced
1 teaspoon Continental Beef Stock powder
½ cup water
2 teaspoons crushed garlic
2 fresh capsicums, cut into strips
1 dessertspoon ground ginger
55 mL hot water
150 grams low-fat natural yoghurt
rock salt and cracked black pepper to taste

Method

1 Place spices in a Teflon frypan, dry-frying for 5 minutes over a gentle heat.
2 In a separate Teflon frypan, brown the meat by dry-frying and then remove to a plate.
3 Add the onions to the meat frypan and cook in stock and water for 5 minutes. Add spices, garlic and capsicum.
4 Cook for a further 5 minutes. Return meat to the pan.
5 Mix the water and yoghurt and add salt. Add to the meat. Cover the frypan and simmer for 2 hours on a low heat.
6 After 2 hours remove the lid and continue to cook for 15 minutes to reduce the sauce slightly.
7 Serve with jasmine rice and fruit. (No rice in the evening!)

Meatloaf with Barbecue Sauce

B   L   D

Medium Protein/Small Carbohydrate
60 minutes to make (including baking time)
Serves 4 adults

Ingredients

750 grams very lean minced beef
3 eggs
3 heaped tablespoons cornflour (a little extra if necessary)
2 heaped tablespoons breadcrumbs
4 tablespoons tomato paste
2 tablespoons Worcestershire sauce
2 tablespoons Fountain Thick Teriyaki Sauce
1 tablespoon Maggi Seasoning Sauce
1 tablespoon spaghetti bolognaise herbs
3 teaspoons dry or 2 of fresh parsley, chopped
1 large onion, chopped finely and 1 large carrot, grated finely
2 teaspoons Continental French Onion Soup Mix
½ teaspoon rock salt and ½ teaspoon cracked black pepper

Method

1 Preheat oven to 180°C (350°F).
2 Mix all ingredients except breadcrumbs. If mixture is too wet, keep adding cornflour.
3 Roll mixture in breadcrumbs. Work until mixture sits firm and is well covered. Sprinkle with salt and pepper.
5 Place the meatloaf on a rack and put the rack in a pan. Cover with foil and cook on the oven for 25 minutes.
6 Remove foil and continue cooking for another 25 minutes.
7 Serve with barbecue gravy: 2 tablespoons low joule beef Gravox, 2 tablespoons tomato sauce, 1 tablespoon Worcestershire sauce and 1 cup of water, stirred in a Teflon pan on a low–medium heat. Add water if necessary.

Lamb

Baked Lamb with Rosemary

Oriental Lamb

Irish Stew with Dumplings

Lamb Curry

Lebanese Green Bean Stew

Baked Lamb with Rosemary

B L D

Medium Protein/Medium Fibrous/ Medium Starchy Carbohydrate
2 hours to make (including baking time)
Serves at least 4 adults

Ingredients

1 medium lean leg of lamb
1 dessertspoon 100% fruit strawberry jam
2 teaspoons rosemary, dried
6 bay leaves
rock salt and cracked black pepper to taste
6 medium potatoes
1 large sweet potato
1 large parsnip
½ butternut pumpkin

Method

1 Preheat the oven to 180°C (350°F).
2 Place lamb in baking dish with *no* oil. Spread jam over the leg. Then sprinkle with rosemary, bay leaves, salt and pepper.
3 Cook halfway with the lid on (approximately 45 minutes). Then in two separate baking dishes, spread out the washed, peeled and cut vegetables, also in *no* oil.
4 Cook for 20 minutes uncovered.
5 Add vegies to lamb. Continue cooking lamb and vegies, uncovered, for 20 minutes. Remove lamb when brown and crisp. Turn vegies over.
6 Turn oven to 220°C (425°F), to brown vegies. Turn when brown.
7 Serve with honey carrots, boiled peas, Gravox low joule gravy and a side salad.

Oriental Lamb

B L D

Medium Protein/Medium Fibrous Carbohydrate
40 minutes to make
Serves 4 adults

Ingredients

500 grams very lean strips of lamb (fillet is good)
1 large onion, finely sliced
1/2 cup celery, sliced
2 tablespoons water
1 cup mushrooms, sliced
2 tablespoons soy sauce
5 teaspoons cornflour
1 large clove garlic, crushed
1 punnet cherry tomatoes
2 cups snow peas
1/2 teaspoon Continental Beef Stock powder

Method

1 Using a large preheated Teflon frypan, sear the lamb then remove from heat and place onto a dish.
2 In a large saucepan, add onion, celery and water and cook on high for 10 minutes.
3 Add lamb and remaining ingredients except tomatoes and snow peas. Stir in gently.
4 Cover with a lid and simmer until meat has cooked through, approximately 10 more minutes.
5 Add snow peas and tomatoes. Cook for 5–7 minutes.
6 Drain off 1 cup of liquid into a small saucepan. Cook on high for approximately 5 minutes. Put all other ingredients in a container with the meat, ready for serving.
7 Pour the sauce over the lamb and vegetables. Serve.

Irish Stew with Dumplings

B   L   D

Medium Protein/Medium Starchy/
Small Fibrous Carbohydrate
2¹/₂ hours to make (including 2 hours simmering time)
Serves at least 4 adults

Ingredients

2 tablespoons plain flour
1 dessertspoon chicken salt
1 kilo very lean lamb
1 large onion, sliced
2 large carrots, sliced
2 medium leeks, washed and sliced
rock salt and cracked black pepper to taste
1 large potato, peeled and sliced
1 tablespoon barley
1¹/₄ L hot water
For the dumplings
110 grams self-raising flour
1 tablespoon fresh parsley, chopped
1 egg (you may not need all of it)

Method

1 Mix flour with chicken salt. Dip the meat in the mixture.
2 Put a layer of meat in the bottom of a large Teflon pan, with some of the onions, carrots, leeks and potatoes. Season with salt and pepper. Add more meat and continue layering the ingredients until everything is in.
3 Sprinkle the barley and pour the hot water over it and bring to simmering point. Spoon off any 'scum' that rises to the surface, then cover the pan with a lid and leave to simmer for 2 hours.

4 Around 15 minutes before cooking time, make the dumplings. Mix the flour with some salt and pepper and the parsley. In a separate bowl, whisk the egg. Add in a little at a time, with some water, until the mixture has a scone-like consistency.

5 When the stew is ready, remove the meat and vegies onto a large, warm serving dish, making sure you leave all the liquid in the pan. Cover the meat with foil.

6 Add some salt and pepper to the pan juices, then bring to the boil quickly.

7 Put the dumplings in, cover and cook for 20 minutes, making sure they don't come off the boil.

8 Serve the meat with the vegies and dumplings, and pour over some of the juices from the pan.

Lamb Curry

B   L   D

Medium Protein/Medium Fibrous Carbohydrate
40 minutes to make (including simmering time)
Serves at least 4 adults

Ingredients

- 2 cups precooked very lean lamb, cubed
- 2 medium-sized Granny Smith apples, peeled, cored and finely sliced
- 1 small tin peeled whole tomatoes (no oil)
- 2 dessertspoons chutney
- 1 dessertspoon tomato sauce
- 2 teaspoons Worcestershire sauce
- 1 teaspoon lemon juice
- 1/2 teaspoon lemon rind, finely grated
- 2 teaspoons curry powder
- 1 tablespoon low joule beef Gravox
- 1/4 cup cold water

Method

1 Place all ingredients except the Gravox and water into a large Teflon frypan.
2 Simmer on low–medium heat with a lid on for 30 minutes.
3 In a separate bowl, mix the Gravox with the water, then pour into frypan, stirring constantly.
4 Replace lid and continue to simmer for another 5 minutes.
5 Serve over fluffy rice for lunch, or with a side salad if you are eating this meal for dinner.

Lebanese Green Bean Stew

B L D

Medium Protein/Small Fibrous Carbohydrate
2¹/₂ hours to make (including simmering time)
Serves at least 4 adults

Ingredients

500 grams green string beans
500 grams very lean lamb, cubed
several meat bones (no fat)
1¹/₂ cups onions, chopped
1¹/₂ teaspoons salt
¹/₂ teaspoon pepper
¹/₂ teaspoon mixed spices
2 tablespoons tomato paste blended with 2¹/₂ cups water
2 cloves garlic
1 teaspoon ground coriander

Method

1 String the beans. Leave whole or slice down the centre.
2 In a large Teflon frypan, simmer the meat, bones and onions.
3 Mix in the beans and fry for a few minutes.
4 Add the salt, pepper and mixed spices, then pour in the tomato paste or soup.
5 Bring to the boil, cover and simmer slowly until the meat is very tender.
6 Crush the garlic with a pinch of salt and the coriander, and cook lightly in a small Teflon frypan, adding a sprinkle of water to stop any sticking. Cook until garlic smells sweet.
7 Stir this mixture into the cooked stew.
8 At lunch serve with Rice Pilaf. If you have this meal for dinner, serve with lightly steamed broccoli and carrots.

Pork

Sweet and Sour Pork

Spicy Grilled Pork

Pork in Black Bean Sauce

Italian Marinated Pork

Speedy Pork Chow Mein

Sweet and Sour Pork

B L D

Medium Protein/Small Fibrous Carbohydrate
40 minutes to make
Serves 4 adults

Ingredients

500 grams very lean fillet of pork, cut into strips
440 gram tin of unsweetened pineapple pieces (drain
  and keep juice)
1 cup bamboo shoots (optional)
1 large red capsicum, chopped
2 sticks celery, chopped
1/2 cup water
1/4 cup white wine
2 tablespoons tomato sauce
1 tablespoon cornflour
1/2 cup spring onions, chopped

Method

1 Sear the pork in a large Teflon frypan until just golden, then
  put aside.
2 Using a large saucepan, add all the ingredients except the
  cornflour, pineapple juice and bamboo shoots.
3 In a separate bowl, dissolve the cornflour in the pineapple
  juice, then add to the saucepan.
4 Half-cook the contents of the saucepan on medium heat.
5 Add the pork and the bamboo shoots and cook for a further
  10 minutes with the lid on.
6 Serve over fluffy rice for lunch or on its own if you're eating
  this meal for dinner.

B   L   D

Spicy Grilled Pork

Medium Protein
30 minutes to make (and has to be refrigerated overnight)
Serves at least 4 adults

Ingredients

400 grams natural low-fat yoghurt
¼ cup French mustard (no oil)
pinch ground allspice
rock salt and cracked black pepper to taste
750 grams very lean pork fillet, cubed
6 metal or 6 wooden skewers (soaked for at least 2 hours in water)

Method

1 In a large bowl combine half the yoghurt with the mustard and seasonings.
2 Add meat and stir well until thoroughly coated. Cover and refrigerate overnight.
3 Thread meat onto 6 skewers and grill for 15–20 minutes.
4 In a saucepan blend the remaining yoghurt with leftover marinade and heat gently. Make sure it doesn't boil.
5 Serve kebabs on a bed of boiled rice, covered with the yoghurt sauce. If you're eating this meal for dinner, omit the rice and serve with the sauce and a salad.

Pork in Black Bean Sauce

B   L   D

Medium Protein/Small Fibrous Carbohydrate
40 minutes to make
Serves at least 4 adults

Ingredients

500 grams very lean fillet of pork, cut into strips
3 cloves garlic, crushed
1 apple, peeled and sliced
1 medium onion, sliced
$\frac{1}{4}$ cup black beans
2 tablespons soy suace
1 tablespoon honey
1 tablespoon sherry or dry white wine
$\frac{1}{2}$ cup water
rock salt and cracked black pepper to taste

Method

1 Place the pork in a large Teflon frypan and cook until just brown.
2 Combine all the other ingredients in a large bowl.
3 Pour over the pork and cook with the lid on for a further 30 minutes on low–medium heat.
4 Serve with rice if eating for lunch, or with some lightly steamed Asian vegetables for dinner.

Italian Marinated Pork

B L D

Medium Protein/Small Fibrous Carbohydrate
1 hour to make (including simmering time)
Serves at least 4 adults

Ingredients

1 long pork fillet, trimmed of fat
2 large onions, finely grated
1 large clove garlic, crushed
2 teaspoons Continental Chicken Stock powder
$\frac{1}{2}$ cup water
$\frac{1}{2}$ cup white wine
4 medium carrots, finely grated
1 cup peas
1 tin peeled whole tomatoes, drained
1 teaspoon oregano
rock salt and cracked black pepper to taste

Method

1 In a large Teflon frypan with the lid on, simmer the pork, onions, garlic, stock, water and wine.
2 After around 20 minutes, when the pork is cooked, lift the pork out onto a dish.
3 Add the other ingredients to the pan juices and simmer for 30 minutes with the lid on.
4 Cut the pork into 1-inch slices and return to the simmering sauce. Continue cooking for another 10 minutes.
5 Serve hot with lightly steamed green vegetables.

B   L   D

Speedy Pork Chow Mein

Medium Protein/Small Starchy/
Small Fibrous Carbohydrate
45 minutes to make
Serves at least 4 adults

Ingredients

500 grams very lean pork mince
1 onion, finely chopped
1 cup cooked white rice
2½ cups of water
1 tablespoon Continental Chicken Stock powder
½ cup rice noodles, no oil
1 tablespoon curry powder
¼ cup finely chopped spring onions
4 cups finely shredded cabbage
440 gram tin pineapple pieces, drained
¼ cup freshly chopped chives

Method

1 Combine all the ingredients except the cabbage, pineapple and chives, in a large Teflon frypan.
2 Stir well until pork is cooked thoroughly, then add the cabbage and pineapple.
3 Cook for a further 15 minutes or so, or until the noodles and all other ingredients are soft.
4 Serve hot with a crusty bread roll for lunch, or on Junk Day in a large lettuce cup for dinner.

Vegetarian

Vegie and Lentil Soup

Stuffed Zucchini

Lentil and Vegetable Moussaka

Vegetarian Shepherd's Pie

Lentil and Rice Pilaf

Vegie and Lentil Soup

B L D

Small Protein/Medium Fibrous Carbohydrate
2 hours to make (including simmering time)
Serves at least 4 adults

Ingredients

1 large onion, chopped
1 large clove garlic, crushed
2 tablespoons soy sauce
1 cup lentils
4 cups water
2 teaspoons Continental Vegetable Stock powder
3 medium carrots, chopped
2 celery stalks, chopped
1 cup cauliflower
2 teaspoons fresh coriander, chopped
rock salt and cracked black pepper to taste
2 teaspoons curry powder (or to taste)
1 cup Carnation Evaporated Skim Milk

Method

1 In a large saucepan, sauté the onion and garlic in soy sauce.
2 Soak the lentils in water for 10 minutes.
3 Add all ingredients except curry powder and evaporated milk.
4 Simmer for 90 minutes on a very low heat.
5 When completely mushy, blend.
6 Add evaporated milk, curry powder and coriander.
7 Serve piping hot with crunchy side salad. Add a bread roll if you're eating this meal for lunch.

Stuffed Zucchini

B L D

Medium Protein/Medium Fibrous Carbohydrate
60 minutes to make
Serves 4 adults

Ingredients

4 medium zucchini
1 teaspoon Continental Beef Stock powder
½ cup water
250 grams mushrooms, finely chopped
1 medium onion, roughly chopped
2 medium tomatoes, roughly chopped
1 celery stalk, sliced
½ teaspoon sweet paprika
rock salt and cracked black pepper to taste

Method

1 Slice the zucchini in half lengthways and scoop out the seeds and flesh.
2 In a large Teflon frypan, cook the stock and water until simmering. Add the mushrooms and cook until lightly browned.
3 Add the remaining ingredients and simmer for 5 minutes.
4 Spoon the mixture into the zucchini shells and place them on a Teflon baking tray.
5 Bake at 200°C (400°F) for 45 minutes, or until tender.

Lentil and Vegetable Moussaka

B L D

Small Protein/Medium Fibrous Carbohydrate
60 minutes to make
Serves 4 adults

Ingredients

50 grams whole green or brown lentils
110 mL water
1 medium eggplant, cut into small cubes
2 dessertspoons Continental Beef Stock powder
1 1/2 cups of water
1 large onion, finely chopped
110 grams red capsicum, finely chopped
1 large clove garlic, crushed
4 tablespoons red wine
1 tablespoon tomato purée
1/4 teaspoon ground cinnamon
1 dessertspoon chopped parsley
rock salt and cracked black pepper to taste
For the Topping
2 eggs (only 1 yolk)
4 tablespoons natural, low-fat yoghurt
2 teaspoons grated parmesan cheese
1/4 teaspoon ground nutmeg

Method

1 Soften the lentils in the water (no salt).
2 Preheat the oven to 180°C (350°F).
3 Prepare the eggplant cubes. Place them in a colander, sprinkle them with salt and cover with a plate weighed down with a heavy object. Leave them to bleed for 20 minutes or so, then rinse and squeeze them dry in a clean tea towel.

4 Pour half the stock and half the water into a medium-sized Teflon frypan and cook the onion and capsicum until softened (around 10 minutes).

5 Remove them and place on a plate.

6 Using the remaining stock and water, cook the eggplant in the same frypan. It will take around 10 minutes to soften.

7 Add the capsicum, and cook for a minute, then add the onion and garlic.

8 In a separate bowl, mix the wine and tomato purée with the cinnamon and parsley. Pour this into the vegetable mixture. Stir in the softened lentils, and add salt and pepper.

9 Stir and combine thoroughly, then spoon everything into an ovenproof dish.

10 Beat all the topping ingredients in a separate bowl.

11 Pour topping mixture over the vegetables.

12 Bake in the oven for 30 minutes or until the top is puffy and golden.

Vegetarian Shepherd's Pie

B L D

Medium Protein/Medium Starchy Carbohydrate
90 minutes to make
Serves 4 adults

Ingredients

175 grams whole brown or green lentils
110 grams split green or yellow peas
575 mL hot water
1 dessertspoon Continental Vegetable Stock powder
1 cup water
2 celery stalks, chopped
1 medium onion, chopped
2 medium carrots, chopped
1/2 medium green capsicum, chopped
1 large clove garlic, crushed
1/2 teaspoon dried mixed herbs
1/4 teaspoon cayenne pepper
rock salt and cracked black pepper to taste
1 small tin peeled whole tomatoes
For the Topping
1 small onion, chopped
1 teaspoon Continental Chicken Stock powder
1/2 cup water
700 grams boiled potatoes
2 tablespoons skim milk
2 teaspoons parmesan cheese, grated

Method

1 Wash then simmer the lentils and split peas in a large, covered saucepan for around 45–60 minutes, or until the peas and lentils have absorbed the water and are soft.

2 Preheat the oven to 190°C (375°C).

3 Simmer the stock and water in a large Teflon pan. Add the celery, onion, carrots and capsicum. Cook gently until softened, adding a little more water if necessary.

4 Mash a little. Add to lentil mixture. Then add the garlic, herbs, spices, salt and pepper. Spoon the mixture into a large pie dish. Arrange the sliced tomatoes on top.

5 For the topping; sauté the onion in the stock and water in a small Teflon frypan.

6 Mash the potatoes, then add the sautéd ingredients and mix well.

7 Season with salt and pepper, then spread on top of the ingredients in the pie dish.

8 Bake for about 20 minutes or until the top is lightly browned.

9 Serve with some tomato sauce or appropriate chutney and a light crunchy green salad, with a no oil dressing.

Lentil and Rice Pilaf

B L D

Medium Protein/Medium Starchy Carbohydrate
60 minutes to make
Serves 6–8 adults

Ingredients

1³/₄ cups lentils
2 large onions
splash of cold water
2 cups rice, washed and drained
1 tablespoon salt
soy sauce to taste

Method

1 Wash the lentils well.
2 Slice onions very finely, and cut into half-circles.
3 Toss into a hot, medium-sized Teflon frypan, and keep tossing until golden brown. Splash drops of cold water over to help the onions brown, but be careful not to add too much water.
4 Remove half the onions from the pan and place on a side plate.
5 In a large saucepan, boil the lentils in water until nearly tender, approximately 20–25 minutes.
6 Mix in the rice and bring back to the boil.
7 Reheat the remaining stock with water until really hot, then toss in the remaining onions. Pour them onto the boiling lentils and rice.
8 Add salt, cover tightly, turn down the heat and simmer slowly until the rice is tender and all the fluid is absorbed, approximately 20 minutes.
9 Serve hot or cold, garnished with the golden brown onion slices. If served cold, accompany with a tossed salad. Add a little soy sauce for a slightly salty taste.

Kids' Meals

recommended by kids!

Hamburgers

Macaroni Cheese

Kids' Spaghetti

Crumbed Fish Fillets

Colourful Chicken Kebabs

B L D

Hamburgers

Medium Protein/Small Starchy/
Small Carbohydrate
20 minutes to make
Serves 4 kids

Ingredients

200 grams very lean beef, minced
1 small onion
1 medium tomato
some interesting lettuce (raddichio, butter, cos)
4 slices beetroot
tomato sauce
4 hamburger buns

Method

1 Heat a large Teflon frypan on high.
2 Make the mince into four even patties and put them into the pan.
3 Cut the onion into 3 mm slices, but do not separate rings.
4 Cook them in the pan with the mince.
5 Turn the patties after 5–7 minutes.
6 Split and toast the hamburger buns.
7 When patties are cooked, remove and place neatly on half of the bun. Top with onion rings.
8 Add the salad and tomato sauce.
9 Serve staightaway with Cajun Baked Sweet Potato Chips (see p. 196).

B   L   D

Macaroni Cheese

Large Carbohydrate
20 minutes to make
Serves 4 kids

Ingredients

2 cups uncooked macaroni elbows or bowties
4 cups water
pinch salt
2 packets Continental Cheese Sauce packet mix
skim milk (as directed on back of the packet, plus a little extra)

Method

1 Using a medium-sized saucepan, cook the macaroni in slightly salted water.
2 In a small Teflon saucepan, mix the cheese sauce with milk as directed on packet.
3 Keep adding milk as you need it. Make sure the sauce isn't too thick.
4 When macaroni is cooked, after 15 minutes, remove from heat, drain and rinse well.
5 Empty macaroni into a dish and pour the cheese sauce over.

Kids' Spaghetti

B   L   D

Medium Protein/Medium Carbohydrate
60 minutes to make
Serves 4 kids

Ingredients

¼ packet thin spaghetti noodles (or any other interesting
type of pasta)
4 cups water
pinch salt
250 grams very lean beef, minced
1 small tin whole peeled tomatoes (no oil added)
2 teaspoons mixed herbs
1 teaspoon Continental Beef Stock powder

Method

1 Using a large frypan, cook the mince.
2 Add tomatoes, stock and herbs.
3 Reduce heat to very low, place a lid on the frypan, and leave
  simmering for 45 minutes.
4 When the sauce is nearly ready, cook the spaghetti noodles
  in a large saucepan filled with slightly salty water.
5 When spaghetti is cooked (after 15 minutes), remove from
  heat, drain and rinse well.
6 Empty into a serving dish. Pour sauce over and mix in.
7 Serve hot with a small, simple salad of lettuce, carrots and
  tomato.

Crumbed Fish Fillets

B   L   D

Large Protein/Small Starchy Carbohydrate
20 minutes to make
Serves 4 kids

Ingredients

4 medium white fish fillets (as boneless as possible)
1 cup cornflour
1 cup breadcrumbs
2 eggs
rock salt and cracked black pepper to taste
4 small lemon wedges

Method

1 Wash the fillets well.
2 Preheat a large Teflon frypan on high.
3 Prepare 2 pieces of greaseproof paper, 1 with cornflour, the other with breadcrumbs.
4 Whisk eggs with salt and pepper to taste, in a small bowl.
5 Roll fillets in the cornflour, then dip well in the egg mixture then roll straight in the breadcrumbs.
6 Place fillets in the hot frypan, watching carefully that they don't burn. Reduce the heat immediately, and place the lid on top.
7 After a couple of minutes, turn fillets over very carefully with a spatula and keep cooking until brown.
8 Sprinkle in a little water, for extra moisture, which also helps the fish to brown slightly.
9 Serve hot with some Creamy Mashed Potatoes (see p. 199), steamed fibrous vegetables, and a lemon wedge on the side.

Colourful Chicken Kebabs

Medium Protein/Medium Fibrous Carbohydrate
20 minutes to make
Serves 4 kids

Ingredients

½ cup oyster sauce
3 single chicken breast fillets
1 large carrot
2 pineapple rings
½ small green capsicum
1 small tomato
8 kebab skewers

Method

1 Wash and trim the chicken of all fat, and cut into bite-sized cubes.
2 Marinate the chicken in the oyster sauce for around 10 minutes.
3 Cut all the fruit and vegetables into bite-sized pieces.
4 Heat a large Teflon frypan on high.
5 Place all the bite-sized pieces, including the chicken, on the kebabs, to make them colourful and interesting.
6 When the pan is hot, toss in the kebabs, four at a time. Turn them as they cook.
7 Remove when cooked and serve with a crunchy salad.

Soups

Pumpkin, Parsnip and Tomato

Chicken and Corn

Leek, Onion and Potato

Minestrone

Chunky Homestyle Beef and Vegie

Pumpkin, Parsnip and Tomato

Medium Fibrous Carbohydrate
25 minutes to make
Serves 4 adults

Ingredients

1 medium–large parsnip
½ butternut pumpkin
4 ripe tomatoes
1 teaspoon dried mixed herbs
1 teaspoon Continental Chicken Stock powder
rock salt and cracked black pepper to taste
a little low-fat sour cream (only if it's Junk Day)
fresh chives, finely chopped, for garnish

Method

1 Remove skin from pumpkin and parsnip.
2 Chop pumpkin, parsnip and tomatoes into chunks.
3 Steam the pumpkin and parsnip in a large saucepan.
4 When cooked, place all ingredients into a large saucepan with 2 tablespoons of water.
5 Simmer on a very low temperature until the tomatoes are cooked.
6 Blend all the ingredients until it reachs a soup consistency.
7 If you've been good all week, you may add two teaspoons of low-fat sour cream or yoghurt and a sprinkle of chives.
8 Serve with a hot crunchy bread roll (no butter).

Chicken and Corn

B L D

Medium Protein/Small Fibrous Carbohydrate
50 minutes to make
Makes 10–12 Servings

Ingredients

6 half chicken fillet breasts, finely chopped
10 cups water
1 small onion, roughly chopped
2 slices 98% fat-free smoked ham, finely chopped
1 knot root ginger (about 1 inch long), finely chopped
6 large stalks spring onions, finely chopped
1 large tin corn nibblets
3 tablespoons cornflour
⅓ cup water
2 teaspoons soy sauce
1 egg

Method

1 Place chicken in a large saucepan with the water.
2 Bring to the boil and simmer on a low heat for approximately 40 minutes or until chicken is cooked.
3 Add all other ingredients except cornflour, water, soy sauce and egg. Bring to the boil.
4 In a small container, mix cornflour and water to a smooth paste, add to soup and let simmer, stirring for 3 minutes.
5 Add soy sauce.
6 In a small container, beat the egg lightly with a fork, then stir into the soup.
7 Serve piping hot with a sprinkle of salt and pepper.

Leek, Onion and Potato

B L D

Small Fibrous/Medium Starchy Carbohydrate
45 minutes to make
Makes 4–6 Servings

Ingredients

4 large leeks
2 medium potatoes, peeled and diced
1 medium onion, finely chopped
2 teaspoons fresh chives, finely chopped
1 teaspoon Continental Chicken Stock powder
1 L water
rock salt and cracked black pepper to taste
325 mL skim milk

Method

1 Remove outer layer of leeks, chop finely, wash thoroughly and drain well.
2 In a large saucepan, add leeks, potatoes, onion, stock, and half a cup of water. Stir them with a wooden spoon so everything is coated with the chicken stock.
3 Add salt and pepper, then cover and let the vegetables sweat over a very low heat for 15 minutes.
4 Add the stock and milk, bring to simmering point, put the lid back on and let the soup simmer very gently for a further 20 minutes or until the vegetables are very soft. Be careful not to overheat or boil over.
5 If you don't like chunky soup, use a liquidiser to purée the ingredients.
6 Stir in chopped chives and serve nice and hot with a fresh bread roll.

B L D

Minestrone

Small Protein/Medium Fibrous/
Medium Starchy Carbohydrate
45 minutes to make
Makes 10–12 Servings

Ingredients

2 potatoes with the skin on, roughly chopped
4 carrots, peeled and finely sliced
3 onions, roughly chopped
1 teaspoon crushed garlic
1 medium tin red kidney beans (no oil)
1 teaspoon Continental Chicken Stock and ½ cup water
14 cups Continental Beef Stock (6 teaspoons stock and 14 cups hot water)
1 large tin peeled tomatoes
4 celery stalks, finely sliced
3 slices 98% fat-free smoked ham, roughly chopped
1 cup macaroni
1 tablespoon chopped parsley
½ teaspoon basil
rock salt and cracked black pepper to taste
1 egg

Method

1 Sauté the vegetables and ham with the chicken stock in a large saucepan. Add beef stock, beans and tomatoes.
2 Bring to the boil, cover and simmer for 30 minutes.
3 Add macaroni and simmer uncovered, until tender.
4 Beat the egg lightly with a fork and stir into the soup.
5 Serve with a sprinkle of parsley and salt and pepper.

Chunky Homestyle Beef and Vegie

B   L   D

Medium Protein/Medium Fibrous Carbohydrate
Make overnight
Makes 10–12 Servings

Ingredients

1 teaspoon Continental Beef Stock powder
1 cup barley
1 kilo very lean beef, cubed
4 carrots, roughly grated
2 turnips, roughly grated
1 small swede, roughly grated
1 large leek, roughly chopped
1 cup chopped celery
½ cup fresh parsley, finely chopped
1 L water

Method

1 In a really large cooking pot, place the stock, half the vegetables, barley and water.
2 Cook for 1–1½ hours or until the meat is tender.
3 Leave overnight for fat to set. It will do this best in the fridge.
4 Skim any fat off the top of the soup the next morning.
5 Add the rest of the ingredients and simmer for another hour, or until barley is nice and soft.
6 Serve piping hot with a crunchy roll – no butter!

Salads

Italian Tomato

Coleslaw

Chinese Greens

Waldorf

Tabbouleh

B   L   D

Italian Tomato

Large Fibrous Carbohydrate
10 minutes to make
Serves 2 adults

Ingredients

2 large tomatoes, sliced
2 large zucchini, sliced
1 large purple onion, sliced
a few fresh basil leaves
rock salt and cracked black pepper to taste
1 cup Kraft Italian dressing (no oil)

Method

1 Using a glass salad bowl, alternately layer all the vegetables and basil leaves.
2 Pour the salad dressing over everything.
3 Add salt and pepper to taste.
4 You may prefer to remove basil leaves before serving!

B L D

Coleslaw

Large Fibrous Carbohydrate
15 minutes to make
Serves 4 adults

Ingredients

$1/2$ cup carrots, shredded
$1/4$ cup white onion, finely chopped
1 cup mixed red and green cabbage, shredded
2 teaspoons parsley, finely chopped
$1/4$ cup brown vinegar
$1/4$ cup Kraft Italian dressing (no oil)
1 dessertspoon honey
sprinkle cracked black pepper

Method

1 Combine vegetables in a large mixing bowl.
2 Mix vinegar, dressing, honey and pepper in a separate, smaller bowl.
3 Pour liquid ingredients over vegetables and mix well.
4 Cover and chill.

B L D

Chinese Greens

Large Fibrous Carbohydrate
10 minutes to make
Serves 4 adults

Ingredients

2 cups chopped Chinese green vegetables
2 cups fresh spinach leaves
1 cup fresh bamboo shoots
1 cup thinly sliced radishes
1/2 cup mushrooms
1 punnet cherry tomatoes
1/4 cup Kraft Italian dressing (no oil)
3 tablespoons Fountain Honey and Soy Sauce (no oil)
cracked black pepper to taste

Method

1 Thoroughly wash and drain all green vegetables, remove all stems, then place in large glass salad bowl.
2 Add radishes, mushrooms, tomatoes and bamboo shoots.
3 Mix dressing, honey and soy sauce and pepper in small bowl.
4 Pour dressing over salad and toss well.

Waldorf

B L D

Large Fibrous Carbohydrate
10 minutes to make
Serves 4 adults

Ingredients

1 tablespoon of lemon juice
3 large red apples, washed and diced
1½ cups celery, washed and diced, unstrung
¼ cup raisins
1 Danone Vanilla Diet Lite vanilla flavoured yoghurt
parsley for garnish

Method

1 Place apples in a medium-sized glass salad bowl.
2 Squeeze lemon juice over apples to prevent discolouring.
3 Add remaining ingredients and toss well.
4 Cover and chill before serving.

B   L   D

Tabbouleh

Medium Fibrous Carbohydrate
1¹/₂ hours to make
Serves 4 adults

Ingredients

¹/₂ cup instant burghul (cracked wheat)
8–10 spring onions
2 teaspoons salt
¹/₄ teaspoon black pepper
¹/₄ teaspoon mixed spices
5 cups very finely chopped parsley
¹/₄ cup very finely chopped fresh mint *or* 2 teaspoons dried mint
3 large tomatoes, finely chopped
¹/₄ cup lemon juice
¹/₄ cup Salad Magic No Oil Mediterranean Dressing

Method

1 Wash the burghul and drain well by squeezing out excess water with cupped hands.
2 Place in a bowl and refrigerate for at least 1 hour.
3 Trim the spring onions, leaving about 20 cm of green.
4 Finely chop the white of the spring onions and mix it into the drained burghul with the salt, pepper and spices.
5 Finely chop the green of the spring onions and place it with parsley, mint and tomatoes on top of the burghul mixture. Set aside in the refrigerator until ready to serve.
6 Just before serving, add the lemon juice and dressing and toss well. Add salt and lemon juice to taste.

Vegetables

Honey Carrots

Super Stir Fry

Corn and Sweet Potato Whip

Barbecued Italian Peppers

Ratatouille

B L D

Honey Carrots

Medium Fibrous Carbohydrate
20 minutes to make
Serves 4 adults

Ingredients

³/₄ cup water
8 medium carrots, peeled and cut diagonally, 1cm thick
³/₄ teaspoon ground cumin
¹/₂ teaspoon fresh ginger, crushed
¹/₄ teaspoon ground coriander
¹/₈ teaspoon cayenne pepper
1 tablespoon honey
2 teaspoons lemon juice

Method

1 Using a medium-sized saucepan, boil water.
2 When boiling, add everything except honey and lemon juice.
3 Reduce the heat and simmer for around 10 minutes.
4 Add lemon juice and honey.
5 Turn up heat and cook until all liquid has evaporated and carrots are soft (around 5 minutes).

B   L   D

Super Stir Fry

Large Fibrous Carbohydrate
15 minutes to make
Serves 4 adults

Ingredients

1 medium head of broccoli
1 small head cauliflower
$^1/_2$ red pepper
1 cup snow peas
1 large zucchini, sliced in chunks
2 large carrots, finely sliced
1 medium red onion, finely sliced
1 cup shredded red and white cabbage
$^1/_2$ cup oyster sauce

Method

1 Wash broccoli and cauliflower and prepare into small, bite-sized pieces.
2 Preheat a large Teflon frypan on high then add all the ingredients. Cover with lid.
3 Cook for a couple of minutes, and stir well.
4 After another 5 minutes with the lid on, remove from heat and serve.

B   L   D

Corn and Sweet Potato Whip

Medium Starchy/Medium Fibrous Carbohydrate
30 minutes to make
Serves 4 adults

Ingredients

1 large sweet potato, washed and peeled
2 large potatoes, washed and peeled
1 large tin corn kernels
rock salt and cracked black pepper to taste
fresh parsley

Method

1 Steam the potatoes until soft over a little water in a large saucepan, approximately 15–20 minutes.
2 Drain the corn well.
3 Place the potato and corn in a medium-sized mixing bowl.
4 Using a blender, whip up the vegetables, adding salt and pepper to taste.
5 Garnish with parsley.

B   L   D

Barbecued Italian Peppers

Medium Fibrous Carbohydrate
20 minutes to make
Serves 4 adults

Ingredients

4 large red capsicums, washed
1 cup red wine vinegar
2 tablespoons fresh basil, chopped
salt and pepper to taste

Method

1 Preheat an outdoor barbecue or an indoor health grill until very hot.
2 Place capsicums on grill and turn. Continue turning until skin has blistered and blackened on all sides.
3 Remove and place in a bowl of cold salty water to loosen skins. Carefully remove skins.
4 After removing skins, place in a shallow serving dish.
5 Pour over vinegar, salt and pepper, and sprinkle with basil.
6 Cover and chill.

B L D

Ratatouille

Medium Fibrous Carbohydrate
30 minutes to make
Serves 4 adults

Ingredients

2 large eggplants
3 medium zucchini
1 red and 1 green capsicum, cored, deseeded and chopped
1 large tin whole peeled tomatoes (no oil), chopped
1 tablespoon fresh basil *or* 2 teaspoons dried basil
1 teaspoon Continental Chicken Stock powder
$^3/_4$ cup water
2 large cloves garlic, crushed
2 medium onions, roughly chopped
rock salt and cracked black pepper to taste
fresh basil leaves or parsley to garnish

Method

1 Wipe eggplant, cut into 1 inch slices, then halve each slice.
2 Wipe zucchini and cut into 1 inch slices.
3 Put the whole lot into a colander. Sprinkle generously with salt. Press them down with a plate. Let stand for 1 hour.
4 In a medium Teflon frypan, simmer stock and water. Add onion and garlic. Cook for 12 minutes then add capsicum.
5 Dry zucchini and eggplant in a towel, then add to the pan.
6 Add the basil, salt and pepper. Stir once really well. Simmer very gently with the lid on for around 30 minutes.
7 Now add the tomato. Taste to make sure the seasoning is right. Cook for a further 15 minutes or so with the lid off.
8 Serve hot as a side dish, with a garnish of fresh basil leaves.

Potatoes

Summer Potato Salad

Cajun Baked Sweet Potato Chips

Potatoes au Gratin

Chipped Potato Grits

Creamy Mashed Potatoes

B L D

Summer Potato Salad

Small Protein/Large Carbohydrate
30 minutes to make
Serves 4 adults

Ingredients

1 kilo Pontiac potatoes, washed and cut into small cubes
   (leave skin on)
4 eggs, boiled and roughly chopped
1/2 cup finely chopped fresh parsley
1/2 cup finely chopped fresh chives
1 large stalk of celery, finely chopped
1 large onion, finely chopped
1 cup low-fat natural yoghurt
2 tablespoons Kraft Italian Dressing (no oil)
2 teaspoons mustard powder
1/2 teaspoon rock salt
1/2 teaspoon cracked black pepper

Method

1 Parboil the potatoes, being careful not to cook them until
   they're mushy.
2 Combine all the other ingredients in a mixing bowl and stir well.
3 Place potatoes in a serving dish and add the dressing.
4 Mix and refrigerate.
5 Best served cold.

Cajun Baked Sweet Potato Chips

B L D

Medium Starchy Carbohydrate
30 minutes to make
Serves 4 adults

Ingredients

1 kilo sweet potatoes, washed and cut into chip strips
   (or substitute Pontiac potatoes with skin left on)
3 eggs
rock salt and cracked black pepper to taste
1 small jar Masterfood's Cajun spices

Method

1 Preheat oven to 220°C (425°F).
2 Beat eggs with salt, pepper and Cajun spices.
3 Dip potato chip strips in egg mixture then place on a Teflon tray and place in the oven to bake for 15 minutes.
4 Check them. When they're brown on one side, turn them, adding a little more Cajun spices and salt.
5 When they're cooked through, after about another 15 minutes, remove from oven.
6 Serve and eat straightaway.

Potatoes au Gratin

B   L   D

Large Starchy Carbohydrate
60 minutes to make
Serves 4 adults

Ingredients

1 kilo Pontiac potatoes, washed and cut into very thin slices
   (leave skin on)
2 extra-large onions, cut into fine rings
1/4 cup finely chopped fresh spring onions
1 packet Continental Cheese Sauce mix
750 mL skim milk
4 slices 98% fat-free ham, finely chopped
rock salt and cracked black pepper to taste
1 teaspoon sweet paprika
1/2 teaspoon crushed garlic

Method

1 Preheat the oven to 205°C (400°F).
2 In a large, ovenproof casserole dish, place the potato slices
   and onion rings and mix well with the ham and spring onions.
3 Mix cheese sauce, milk and other ingredients in a separate bowl.
4 Pour sauce over the potato mixture.
5 Place in the oven until potatoes are browned slightly and
   soft, approximately 60 minutes.

Chipped Potato Grits

B   L   D

Large Starchy Carbohydrate
20 minutes to make
Serves 4 adults

Ingredients

1 kilo Pontiac potatoes, washed and cut into very thin slices
(leave skin on)
2 extra-large onions, cut into fine rings
2 teaspoons Continental French Onion Soup mix
$^1\!/_2$ teaspoon dill
2 cups water

Method

1 Place all ingredients in a large Teflon frypan and cover.
2 Allow to cook on a medium-high heat until potatoes are soft.
3 Reduce the heat and allow to simmer while fluids reduce.
4 Add a little water as you go if necessary.
5 Stir so it looks really messy.

B   L   D

Creamy Mashed Potatoes

Large Starchy Carbohydrate
15 minutes to make
Serves 4 adults

Ingredients

1 kilo Pontiac potatoes, cut into quarters (leave skin on)
1 egg
a little skim milk
rock salt and cracked black pepper to taste
¼ cup freshly chopped parsley

Method

1 Boil the potatoes until soft.
2 Drain well and place in bowl ready for mixing.
3 In a separate bowl, whisk the egg.
4 Mash the potatoes dry at first, adding the egg. Then, using an electric mixer, give the potatoes a good mash.
5 Add a little skim milk until the mixture is nice and creamy. Be careful not to add too much. If you do, put in a saucepan on the stove on a medium heat until reduced a little.
6 Add salt and pepper to taste and garnish with parsley.

Pasta

Spaghetti Bolognaise

Fettucine Boscaiola

Fettucine Salmone

Pumpkin Gnocchi with Crabmeat and Cheese Sauce

Tortellini with Chicken and Mushroom Sauce

Spaghetti Bolognaise

B L D

Medium Protein/Large Starchy Carbohydrate
20 minutes to make
Serves at least 4 adults

Ingredients

1 packet spaghetti
500 grams lean beef mince
1 medium onion, chopped
1 teaspoon Continental Chicken Stock powder
1 cup cold water
3 teaspoons dried bolognaise herbs
1/2 teaspoon paprika
1/2 teaspoon crushed garlic
1 teaspoon Bonox
1 tablespoon Gravox Low Joule Beef Gravy powder
1 cup water
250 grams tomato paste
735 grams tomato soup

Method

1 Begin cooking spaghetti in a large saucepan of boiling water, stirring occasionally. Add more water if necessary.
2 In a large Teflon frypan, cook the beef, onion, stock and water on medium–high heat until brown.
3 Turn down heat and add all herbs and garlic. Stir.
4 In a separate bowl, mix the Gravox with 1 cup of water and slowly add to the other ingredients.
6 Turn off stove and cover frypan with a lid.
7 Drain spaghetti and wash thoroughly using a colander.
8 Serve bolognaise sauce on spaghetti piping hot, with a side serve of salad vegetables.

B L D

Fettuccine Boscaiola

Small Protein/Large Starchy Carbohydrate
25 minutes to make
Serves at least 4 adults

Ingredients

1 large packet fettuccine
1 large onion, finely chopped
3 large spring onion stalks, finely chopped
4 slices 98% fat-free smoked ham, finely chopped
1 cup fresh small mushrooms, finely chopped
1 teaspoon Continental Chicken Stock powder
1 teaspoon dried or fresh parsley
1 teaspoon rock salt and cracked black pepper to taste
2 packets Continental Cheese Sauce mix
750 mL skim milk
½ cup water

Method

1 Cook fettuccine in a large saucepan of boiling water, stirring occasionally. Add more water if necessary. Remove from stove before noodles are too soft.
2 In a large Teflon pan, cook onion, spring onions, ham, mushrooms, stock, parsley and water on medium high until browned. Add a little water if necessary. Remove from stove.
3 In a Teflon saucepan, add cheese sauce and half the milk.
4 Stir constantly until sauce thickens, then add the remaining milk until a pancake-type consistency is reached.
5 Drain and rinse fettuccine and return to saucepan.
6 Add ingredients from the frypan, then add cheese sauce. Mix well and transfer to container for serving.
7 Allow to sit. Add more milk, if necessary, as sauce thickens.
8 Serve piping hot with a crunchy Italian roll (no butter!)

B L D

Fettuccine Salmone

Small Protein/Large Starchy Carbohydrate
25 minutes to make
Serves at least 4 adults

Ingredients

1 large packet fettuccine
1 large onion, finely chopped
3 large spring onion stalks, finely chopped
4 slices 98% fat-free smoked ham, chopped
2 packets Continental Cheese Sauce mix
1 teaspoon Continental Chicken Stock powder
1 teaspoon dried or fresh parsley
1 teaspoon dried mixed herbs
1 teaspoon cracked black pepper
1 pinch of rock salt
50 grams smoked salmon
2 tablespoons Kraft Low Fat Thousand Island Dressing
2 tablespoons tomato sauce
1 cup fresh small mushrooms, finely chopped
750 mL skim milk
½ cup cold water

Method

1 Begin cooking fettuccine in a large saucepan of boiling water, stirring occasionally. Add more water if necessary. Remove from stove before noodles are too soft.

2 In a large Teflon frypan, cook the onion, spring onions, ham, mushrooms, stock, parsley and water on medium high temperature until browned. Add a little water if necessary. Remove from the stove.

3 Pour the cheese sauce mix and half of the milk into a small Teflon saucepan.
4 Stir constantly until sauce thickens, then add the remaining milk until a pancake-type consistency is reached.
5 Drain and rinse fettuccine and return to large saucepan.
6 Add the ingredients from the frypan. Add the cheese sauce, salmon, dressing, tomato sauce and mixed herbs.
7 Mix well and transfer to 1 litre container for serving.
8 Allow to sit. Add more milk if necessary as starch begins to thicken sauce.
9 Serve piping hot with a crunchy Italian bread roll (no butter).

B L D

Pumpkin Gnocchi with Crabmeat and Cheese Sauce

Small Protein/Medium Starchy Carbohydrate
15 minutes to make
Serves at least 4 adults

Ingredients

1 packet Lattina fresh pumpkin gnocchi
1 packet Continental Cheese Sauce mix
325 mL skim milk
1 pinch rock salt
1 teaspoon cracked black pepper
1 large can white crabmeat (fresh if available)
1 teaspoon dried or fresh parsley

Method

1 Boil water in a large saucepan, then add the gnocchi. Cook for 5 minutes on high. Ensure you don't overcook. Drain pasta, then wash with cold water.
2 In a small Teflon saucepan, add the cheese sauce mix, milk, salt and pepper.
3 Stir constantly until sauce thickens, adding more milk if necessary.
4 Add the crabmeat to the cooked and thickened cheese sauce, stirring well.
5 Place the pasta in a 1 litre casserole dish. Pour the crabmeat and cheese sauce over pasta and mix well.
6 Allow to sit. Add more milk if necessary as starch begins to thicken.
7 Garnish with parsley and serve piping hot.

B   L   D

Tortellini with Chicken and Mushroom Sauce

Medium Protein/Large Starchy Carbohydrate
25 minutes to make
Serves at least 4 adults

Ingredients

1 packet Fedora cheese and tomato tortellini (no oil added)
6 half chicken breast fillets, cut into bite-sized pieces
1 medium onion, finely chopped
4 large fresh spring onion stalks, finely chopped
4 slices 98% fat-free smoked ham
1 teaspoon Continental Chicken Stock powder
1 teaspoon dried or fresh parsley
1 dessertspoon Dijon seed mustard (no oil)
1 cup fresh mushrooms, finely chopped
1 teaspoon cracked black pepper
large pinch rock salt
1 packet Continental Cheese Sauce mix
1 packet Lawry's Stroganoff Sauce mix
750 mL skim milk

Method

1 Boil water in a large saucepan. Add pasta, and cook for 5–7 minutes on high. Don't overcook. When you drain pasta, rinse with cold water.

2 In a large Teflon frypan, cook the chicken, onion, spring onions, ham, mushrooms, stock, parsley, mustard and water on medium–high temperature until browned. Add a little water if necessary, and remove from the stove.

4 Place the cheese, stroganoff, and half of the milk in a small Teflon saucepan.

5 Stir constantly until sauce thickens, then add the remaining milk until a pancake-type consistency is reached.
6 Add the sauce and pasta to the large frypan, mixing in well.
7 Once heated through, transfer to a $1^{1}/_{2}$ litre container for serving.
8 Allow to sit. Add a little more milk if necessary as starch begins to thicken.
9 Serve piping hot with vegetables.

Rice

Special Fried Rice

Mexican Rice

Rice Pudding

Japanese Rice (Chirashi Zushi)

Rice on the Side

Special Fried Rice

B L D

Small Protein/Large Starchy Carbohydrate
45 minutes to make
Makes 6–8 servings

Ingredients

1 kilo white rice (or brown if you prefer)
1 teaspoon Continental Chicken Stock powder
4 slices 98% fat-free ham, finely chopped
1 large onion, finely chopped
³/₄ cup finely chopped spring onions
¹/₂ cup water
2 eggs, beaten
¹/₄ cup soy sauce
rock salt and cracked black pepper to taste

Method

1 Boil the rice until just cooked.
2 Wash rice thoroughly in a large colander then leave to dry for about half an hour.
3 In a large Teflon frypan, add the stock, ham, onion, spring onions and water and cook until brown. Add a little extra water if necessary.
4 In a small Teflon frypan, add the eggs with soy sauce, stir to blend and cook like an omelette. Chop when cooked.
5 Add rice gradually to frypan ingredients, stirring through.
6 Add the egg and fold through.
7 Add salt and pepper.
8 Serve piping hot, or cold the next day!

Mexican Rice

B L D

Small Fibrous Large Starchy Carbohydrate
45 minutes to make
Serves 4 adults

Ingredients

1 teaspoon Continental Chicken Stock powder
1 cup water
1 small onion, chopped
1 small green capsicum, chopped
2 cups cooked white or brown rice
½ cup corn kernels
½ cup diced tomato
1 cup mild salsa (no oil)

Method

1 Using a large Teflon frypan on a medium heat, simmer ½ teaspoon of stock powder with ½ cup water.
2 Add onion and capsicum and cook until tender.
3 Add corn, tomato, remaining stock and water, and salsa.
4 Cook all ingredients until boiling.
5 Stir in cooked rice, cover with lid, turn off heat and leave sitting for 5 minutes.
6 Great served as a side dish with fish or chicken.

Rice Pudding

B   L   D

Large Carbohydrate
45 minutes to make
Serves 4 adults

Ingredients

250 grams white or brown rice
500 mL skim milk
2 dessertspoons 100 % fruit jam of your choice
½ cup sultanas or raisins (or mixed)
½ teaspoon nutmeg
2 teaspoons vanilla essence
2 slices toasted white bread

Method

1 Preheat the oven at 205°C (400°F).
2 Place the rice, milk, fruit, nutmeg and vanilla essence in a casserole dish.
3 Spread the jam over the bread and cut into bite-sized squares.
4 Place pieces of bread over the top of the mixture so it fits like a lid.
5 Bake in the oven until brown and rice is cooked and thickened, approximately 40 minutes.

Japanese Rice (Chirashi Zushi)

B L D

Medium Protein/Medium Starchy/ Medium Fibrous Carbohydrate
30 minutes to make
Serves 4

Ingredients

375g short-grain white rice
3 cups water
1 small cucumber
1 teaspoon rock salt
6 teaspoons white vinegar (rice if possible)
3½ teaspoons sugar
100 grams white fish fillet
2 eggs, well beaten
90 grams peas, cooked
1 tablespoon shredded preserved ginger
Sauce
2 tablespoons soy sauce
1 tablespoon white vinegar

Method

1 Wash rice, put into a heavy-based saucepan, cover with water and cook, covered, on low heat until tender. Put aside.
2 Wipe cucumber and rub with a little salt. Shred or grate, then marinate in a mixture of 3 teaspoons vinegar and 1 teaspoon sugar.
3 Steam or boil fish fillet until soft, then flake or chop coarsely. Sprinkle with a mixture of 3 teaspoons vinegar, 1½ teaspoons sugar and ½ teaspoon salt.

4 Mix eggs with 1 teaspoon sugar and $\frac{1}{2}$ teaspoon salt and pour into large Teflon pan. Cook until firm, turn and cook other side, then remove and cook.
5 When cool, shred with a sharp knife.
6 For the sauce, mix soy sauce with vinegar and pour into rice and mix in with a chopstick, then fold in fish, cucumber, shredded egg and peas.
7 Garnish with shredded ginger.

Rice on the Side

B   L   D

Medium Starchy/Large Starchy Carbohydrate
20 minutes to make
Serves 4

Ingredients

250 grams brown rice
1½ cups corn kernels, cooked
2 eggs, beaten
1 small onion, finely chopped
soy sauce to taste
cracked black pepper to taste

Method

1 Cook rice until soft, then drain and wash well.
2 Into a large serving dish add the rice, mixed with corn.
3 In a small Teflon pan cook the eggs scrambled style, stirring all the time.
4 Add the onion to the egg and mix well.
5 Add the egg and onion to the rice and corn.
6 Pour a little soy sauce and pepper over the mixture and serve either hot or cold.

Desserts

Chocoholic's Dream

Berry Delight

Banana Split

Honey and Lemon Crêpes

Grapefruit Jelly Halves

Chocoholic's Dream

B L D

Small Protein/Medium Simple Carbohydrate
10 minutes to make
Serves 4 adults

Ingredients

1 tub Street's Too Good To Be True chocolate ice-cream
1 container Nimbin Valley low-fat custard
4 teaspoons Cottee's low joule chocolate topping

Method

1 This dessert is best served in either a tall, clear, dessert balloon or a clear bowl.
2 Spoon in the ice-cream, then layer in the custard, then topping. Repeat until the bowl is full.
3 Sprinkle generously with Ovaltine.

Berry Delight

B L D

Small Protein/Medium Simple Carbohydrate
10 minutes to make
Serves 4 adults

Ingredients

1 container Nimbin Valley low-fat custard
4 dessertspoons Ovaltine
Vitari 99% Frozen Fruit Dessert (any flavour)
fresh mint for garnish
$^1\!/_2$ kilo fresh mixed berries (or any one alone)

Method

1 This dessert is best served in either a tall clear dessert balloon or a clear bowl.
2 First pour in the custard, evenly distributing it over the four dishes or glasses.
3 Sprinkle 1 dessertspoon of Ovaltine over each serving.
4 Tumble in the mixed or single berries, ensuring you fill the dish amply. Do not mix in with the custard.
5 Serve with some Vitari and garnish with a sprig of fresh mint and a large strawberry which has been split on the side.

B   L   D

Banana Split

Small Protein/Medium Starchy Carbohydrate
10 minutes to make
Serves 4 adults

Ingredients

4 large ripe bananas
1 container Nimbin Valley low-fat custard
1 container low-fat natural yoghurt
4 dessertspoons honey
2 dessertspoons raisins

Method

1 Peel then slice the bananas down the centre and place in 4 suitable dishes.
2 Pour the desired amount of yoghurt and custard over them in a messy fashion.
3 Dribble honey over the dish and toss in raisins.
4 Serve with a cup of Ovaltine hot chocolate made with skim milk.

Honey and Lemon Crêpes

B   L   D

Medium Starchy Carbohydrate
20 minutes to make
Serves 4–6 adults

Ingredients

2 cups plain flour
4 cups skim milk
2 eggs
fresh seasonal fruit, roughly chopped
lemon
honey

Method

1 Mix flour, milk and eggs in a bowl until light and airy.
2 In a very hot Teflon pan, pour in enough mixture to form a crêpe the size of a side plate.
3 When air bubbles appear on top of the crêpe and moisture has evaporated, carefully turn crêpe over.
4 After 30 seconds or so, slide crêpe out onto large plate.
5 Place fresh fruit into centre of crêpe, then roll into a loose tube.
6 Serve with honey and lemon.

Grapefruit Jelly Halves

B   L   D

Medium Fibrous Carbohydrate
25 minutes to make and overnight to set
Serves 4 adults

Ingredients

2 large, sweet-smelling grapefruit
1 packet Cottee's low-calorie lemon jelly crystals
water as per the directions on jelly pack
4 dessertspoons low-fat natural yoghurt *or* Danone Diet Lite
 Lemon Sorbet Yoghurt
4 sprigs fresh mint

Method

1 Wash grapefruit and slice in half. Empty the pulp deseed, cut into cubes, and place into a mixing bowl. Be careful not to damage the skin halves.
2 In a separate bowl, mix the jelly crystals and water (less half a cup), as per the directions on the pack.
3 When jelly mix is thoroughly dissolved, add the grapefruit, mixing well.
4 Place the grapefruit-skin halves in suitable bowls, and place in the refrigerator.
5 When the jelly has set, spoon into the skin halves and return to the refrigerator until ready to be served.
6 Serve with a dessertspoon of low-fat yoghurt and topped with a sprig of fresh mint.

Snacks

Savoury Pancakes

Honey and Banana Pikelets

Country Scones

Strawberry, Guava and Banana Toast

Blueberry Protein Cakes

Savoury Pancakes

B L D

Small Protein/Medium Starchy Carbohydrate
20 minutes to make
Serves 2 adults

Ingredients

2 large washed potatoes
1½ cups self-raising flour
1 cup skim milk
2 eggs
4 large spring onions, finely chopped
handful of fresh parsley, finely chopped
1 teaspoon Continental French Onion Soup mix
rock salt and cracked black pepper to taste

Method

1 Grate the potatoes, leaving the skin on.
2 In a large bowl, thoroughly mix all the ingredients, adding the milk a little at a time. Ensure that the consistency is fairly thick.
3 Heat a medium-sized Teflon frypan, making sure it is very hot before you begin to cook.
4 Spoon the mixture into the pan, creating pancakes approximately 10–15 cm in diameter.
5 When one side has browned well, turn and brown the other side. Make sure the middle is cooked right through.
6 Serve with eggs and a sprinkle of fresh parsley and a little salt, for breakfast at any time of the day (not night).
   Note The mixture will spoil quickly, so make sure you cook it straightaway.

Honey and Banana Pikelets

B   L   D

Small Protein/Medium Starchy Carbohydrate
20 minutes to make
Serves 2 adults

Ingredients

1 medium-sized banana
2 eggs
2 tablespoons honey
1½ cups self-raising flour
1–2 cups skim milk
pinch nutmeg
fresh fruit and fruit jams for topping

Method

1 In a small bowl, mash the banana with the eggs and honey.
2 Together in a large bowl, mix all the ingredients well, adding the milk a little at a time. Ensure the consistency remains medium to thick. Try to froth the mixture slightly if possible.
3 Heat a medium-sized Teflon frypan, making sure it is very hot before you begin to cook.
4 Spoon the mixture into the pan to form pikelets approximately 5–10 cm in diameter.
5 When one side has browned well, turn and brown the other side. Make sure the middle is cooked right through.
6 Serve with 100% fruit jams and fresh fruit.

Country Scones

B L D

Medium Starchy Carbohydrate
10 minutes to make
Serves 4 adults

Ingredients

225 grams self-raising flour
pinch of salt
1 egg
150 mL skim milk
a little extra flour
100% fruit jams for topping

Method

1 Preheat the oven to 220°C (425°F).
2 Sift the flour into a large mixing bowl with the salt.
3 In a separate small bowl, whisk the egg.
4 Slowly pour egg into flour mixture, and rub with hands.
5 Knead the mixure to a soft dough, adding a little more milk if it feels at all dry. Be careful not to overhandle.
6 Roll in flour, keeping centre fairly moist. Flatten out until mixture is around 2½ cm thick. Cut into circles using a cutter or the top of a drinking glass.
7 Dust a non-stick baking tray with a little flour.
8 Set the scones around 3 cm apart.
9 Cook for 12–15 minutes, or until they have risen and are just golden brown.
10 Cool on a wire rack and eat slightly warm with some 100% fruit jam.

B   **L**   **D**

Strawberry, Guava and Banana Toast

Medium Starchy Carbohydrate
5 minutes to make
Serves 2 adults

Ingredients

4 slices heavily grained wholemeal and barley bread
Berri Strawberry and Guava 100% fruit jam
1 banana

Method

1 Toast the bread.
2 Spoon the required amount of jam on top.
3 Neatly slice the banana over the jam.
4 Serve hot with tea or coffee.

B   L   D

Blueberry Protein Cakes

Medium Protein
15 minutes to make
Serves 4 adults

Ingredients

1 punnet fresh blueberries
1 cup whey protein concentrate
1 cup self-raising flour
1 egg
1 cup milk

Method

1 In a small Teflon saucepan, lightly simmer the blueberries until soft.
2 Combine all ingredients in a large mixing bowl. The mixture should be of a pancake-like consistency.
3 Preheat a large teflon frypan.
4 Spoon in the mixture, four at a time. Be careful to flip them over before they burn.
5 When the other side has almost cooked though, remove quickly from the pan.
6 Serve straightaway. These go stale after half a day, so only make what you need.

Party
Appetisers

Garlic King Prawns

Cold Dip Platter

San Choy Bow

Pizzettas with Sun-dried Tomatoes

Salmon and Potato Croquettes

Garlic King Prawns

B   L   D

Medium Protein
10 minutes to make
Serves 4 adults

Ingredients

1 teaspoon Continental French Onion Soup mix
¼ cup water
4 teaspoons crushed garlic
1 teaspoon mixed herbs
1 teaspoon sea/rock salt
40 large, fresh, uncooked king prawns, peeled and deveined
½ cup white wine
1 lemon
cracked black pepper to taste

Method

1 In a large Teflon frypan, heat the soup mix, water, garlic, herbs and salt.
2 When the mixture is very hot, add the prawns and white wine, stirring constantly.
3 The prawns will be cooked in just a few minutes. They need to be served immediately with their sauce in a preheated dish with a slice of lemon.

B L D

Cold Dip Platter

Large Fibrous Carbohydrate
10 minutes to make
Serves at least 4 adults

Ingredients

2 medium-sized carrots
2 celery stalks
8 medium-sized mushrooms
$\frac{1}{2}$ red capsicum
$\frac{1}{2}$ green capsicum
1 cup yellow squash
2 small tomatoes
handful of fresh snow peas
1 cup salsa (no oil)
$\frac{3}{4}$ cup Jalna low-fat ricotta cheese
$\frac{1}{4}$ cup sweet mustard pickles
1 cup apple sauce (no sugar added)

Method

1 Wash all the vegetables and slice into finger-sized pieces.
2 Using a large, open platter, arrange the vegetables into their own section.
3 In the middle, place three small bowls containing the salsa, ricotta cheese mixed with sweet mustard pickles and apple sauce.
4 Serve chilled and fresh.

B L D

San Choy Bow

Medium Protein/Medium Fibrous Carbohydrate
20 minutes to make
Serves 4 adults

Ingredients

250 grams very lean beef mince
1 small onion, diced
1 teaspoon garlic salt
1 cup small broccoli heads
1 cup small cauliflowerettes
1 small carrot, shredded
½ cup cabbage, shredded
1 teaspoon Masterfood's Cajun spices
cracked black pepper to taste
4 large, crisp, iceberg lettuce leaves

Method

1 In a hot, medium-sized Teflon frypan, toss the beef, onion and garlic salt.
2 When cooked, add all the vegetables except the lettuce, and cover with a lid. Cook until vegetables are only just soft (should still be very firm).
3 Trim the large lettuce leaves so they resemble the shape of a bowl.
4 Spoon the warm mince mixture into the cold lettuce leaves, sprinkle with pepper, and serve immediately.

Pizzettas with Sun-dried Tomatoes   B   L   D

Small Fibrous/Medium Starchy Carbohydrate
15 minutes to make
Serves 4 adults

Ingredients

1 long French breadstick, cut into 12 pieces
100 grams sun-dried tomatoes (not in oil), chopped
fresh basil
200 grams tomato purée

Method

1 This recipe is really easy. Spread each slice of the French stick with tomato purée.
2 Sprinkle with a little fresh basil.
3 Top with some chopped sun-dried tomatoes.
4 Grill until the sides of the pizzettas are golden brown and serve piping hot.

Salmon and Potato Croquettes

B   L   D

Medium Protein/Medium Starchy Carbohydrate

25 minutes to make
Serves 4 adults

Ingredients

little skim milk
3 medium large washed potatoes
2 small tins Safcol Silver Salmon
1 egg
1 large onion, finely chopped
1 teaspoon Continental French Onion Soup mix
2 large spring onion stalks, finely chopped
2 teaspoons cracked black pepper
1/2 teaspoon rock salt
3 tablespoons cornflour (a little extra if necessary)
1 tablespoon water
1/2 lemon

Method

1 Boil potatoes in water with skin on. When cooked, mash with a little skim milk and put in mixing bowl.
2 Mix salmon, potatoes and remaining ingredients.
3 Take large dessertspoons of mixture and roll in your hands in a croquette shape. Roll it in a little cornflour on a sheet of wax paper. Add enough cornflour so mixture is not too wet.
4 Place the salmon croquettes in a preheated Teflon pan.
5 When they have browned slightly on one side, turn them over, add a tablespoon of water and place a lid on the pan.
6 Watch the croquettes carefully. When they have browned, turn off the heat.
7 Serve hot or cold with a crisp salad and a wedge of lemon.

Chapter 17

Q & A of How and Why

HOW DO I MAINTAIN MY NEW BODY SHAPE?

Now that's an easy question to answer. You just stick with the System. It's important to remember that you can do as much or as little for as long or as short as you wish. If you want to maintain your new improved body shape, all you have to remember are the principles. When you've achieved your goal, your metabolism will be faster, and you can probably afford to occasionally have a couple of Junk Days per week. Because of the foundation you have laid in stripping body fat instead of muscle tissue and water, your weight doesn't pour back on if you go off the rails for a while. Just remember what you have put into achieving your new body shape, and that should be reason enough to keep a close check on what you eat.

HOW CAN SOME PEOPLE BE THIN, YET STILL FAT?

Ever noticed how even the skinniest girl in short shorts can still have dimply, flabby legs? This is because the muscle tissue has been starved by poor nutrition, and by severe lack of exercise. That's why even some bigger women look great, because they are a healthy size, with low body fat. It's the naked you which really counts and shows how healthy you are. It's much better to be a healthy size 10–12 with no cellulite!

HOW DO I USE WEIGHTS WITHOUT GROWING HUGE MUSCLES?

To start with, it is a biological fact that women do not have the capacity to grow huge muscles. The human body needs a great deal of testosterone (most of which is found in men) before it can produce bulging muscles. Even if you are a woman and have a slightly higher than normal level of testosterone, you would need to take mega doses of steroids before you could become huge – not to mention the amount of eating and training you would have to do. So, relax and know that your muscles are only going to become as big and toned as they can naturally (which can be very attractive). After all, it's the size, tone and shape of your body's muscles, along with the amount of body fat on top, which determines your body shape. Having seen the lean, slightly athletic, toned variety, I know which body type I'd be aiming for!

HOW LONG WILL IT TAKE FOR MY METABOLISM TO CHANGE?

The average time it takes for a sluggish metabolism to speed up is approximately 6 to 8 weeks. Of course, your genetics, fitness levels, and how careful you are at following the System will determine how long it takes you personally. The main thing to remember is that if you follow the System, your metabolism will change, so have patience and just keep going until it does!

HOW MANY LOW-CALORIE DRINKS MAY I HAVE EACH DAY?

This depends entirely on you. Water and milk are the only fluids you need, so anything above and beyond is a matter of choice. Some diet drinks can dehydrate you, so ensure you drink enough water to compensate. Again, we're not talking about health here, but we are talking about body shaping, so if, for the time being, by drinking a diet soft drink, it will stop you from eating a bar of chocolate – go for it! Just have these types of drinks in moderation. A great alternative is fresh water with a squeeze of fresh citrus juice.

HOW DO I LOSE THE FAT FROM ONE PART OF MY BODY?

Simple – you can't! Even when you are exercising one particular part of your body in the hopes that you can, you should know that doing the exercise itself is not what's going to get rid of the fat. Exercise speeds your metabolism and toned muscle is what burns fat. So, your body fat will diminish, but reality is that it will probably not go from where you want it to disappear first. Be patient, and it will go in proportion. The best part of following this System is that you will notice body fat gone from places you never thought possible!

fat free forever tips

101 TIPS FOR WEIGHT LOSS

fat free forever tips

The Body
Shaping
Mini
Manual

Dianne Barker

Fat Free Forever Tips is an inspirational and practical companion to the successful *Fat Free Forever!
The Body Shaping System.*

Fat Free Forever Tips will motivate you to change your eating habits overnight. This book will help you lose weight and keep it off.

Available at all good bookstores. ARRP $9.95

Whey Protein Concentrate Body Shaping Food

Due to popular demand, I am including some helpful information on where you can purchase Whey Protein Concentrate products at very reasonable prices. Not only is it the best form of protein for you, it's cheaper than eggs!

"Life-Body Shaping Food"
Pure Whey Protein Concentrate
by Aussie Bodies

available from

All leading health food stores & Supermarkets

or by direct mail

Aussie Bodies
Suites 22–23
170 Forster Road
Mt. Waverley. VIC. 3149
Tel: (613) 9558 9933
Fax: (613) 9558 9952

Testimonials

your say...

I want YOU ...
to contact me...
about the three 'F's!

FEEDBACK!

One of the most encouraging things for an author to receive is feedback — especially when it's positive! I would like to thank those people who have read my book and taken the time to write about the wonderful changes they've experienced (see the following pages). I love getting these letters and want to encourage you to write or fax your comments about how *Fat Free Forever!* has helped change your life.

FOTOS!

If you have any 'before and after' photographs, please send these to me also.

FOOD!

If you have come up with any new ideas and variations to the recipes that I've suggested, please let me know and we may even include your contribution in my next book, *Easy Exercise for Everyone!* (to be published in 1997).

I wrote this book for you and it's important to me that what I'm saying is encouraging, applicable, and that it works (*and we know it does!*), so please feel free to contact me and let me know how you're going.

Dianne Barker
Fat Free Forever!
Reed Books
PO Box 251, Pyrmont, NSW 2009, Australia
Fax: (02) 9549 8950

For lecture and seminar bookings, please contact the above.

Dear Dianne

Just a note to say thank you for Fat Free Forever!
*I'm thrilled to say that your eating plan has worked
absolute wonders for me. I know I'm not supposed to
be weighing myself all the time, but there is now 13
kilograms less of me now that at last November's
seminar! Very exciting and so easy! I remember being
very discouraged ... on the day of the seminar — I was
90.2 kilograms — I looked and felt incredibly fat.
(I'm thirty-seven years old, but for my first twenty-six
years, I looked like a stick. Ate whatever I fancied.
Then came the beginnings of middle-age spread ...
I thought that the spare tyre was there to stay!)*

*I started your plan the day after the seminar, following
just what I recalled of your session ... I've never eaten
so much (quality) food in my life, yet the first 2
kilograms literally fell off in the first week. That was
encouraging. I weaned myself from full cream to Lite
White milk by topping up the old container every time
I used some up. Breakfast is huge! And thank God for
those Danone light yoghurts.*

*After nine weeks (including a huge Junk Day at
Christmas and all those munchies at New Year), I'd
lost a total of 7 kilograms. The next 3 kilograms went
rather slowly, then it all levelled out. About this time,
a local health club slipped a card under my door.
(I don't have a car, so I get in plenty of walking; gyms
aren't me.) However, the card had one of those*

height/weight charts; I worked out I should have been 77 kilograms for my frame and height. I was very, very happy at 80 kilograms, but could I lose that last 3 kilograms?

Then your book came out! With the wonderful cornucopia of recipes within, the remaining weight was gone in a fortnight. I now have two Junk Days per week. My weight is still a steady 77 kilograms ...

By-the-way, a friend recently passed a kidney stone. [Using your book] he has lost 12 kilograms [in ten weeks] and his doctor is flabbergasted. His triglyceride and cholesterol counts are within normal parameters already. He'd been told it would take three years.

Ian McLean, NSW

Dear Dianne

Never before have I written to an author! I just had to on this occasion. I'm a self-confessed diet/health/fitness fanatic. I understand a lot about my body and how it works. Well, I thought I did.

I have just finished reading Fat Free Forever! for the second time in two days. Today I started on the 'system'. I guess I should have waited until I showed a result to write and thank you, but I know I will show a result, so I'm writing to say congratulations in advance.

It's common sense! It's easy!

I work out twice a day… over one-and-a-half hours a day. I eat fat free. I have plateaued. Nothing would kick-start me. My problem area is my tummy and I'm desperate to get rid of it. At thirty-seven and after two Caesareans I know it won't be perfect, but I want it better than it is and I believe I will have it.

I saw your book … and it immediately excited and inspired me, not only to change my eating habits but to source out another gym and have them design a new program for me. Time is something I don't have (like everyone else), so it's really important to get it all right.

Thank you! This makes more sense than anything I've read. I'm going to buy a copy for my mum (who's overweight) and I've been recommending it to all who'll listen — yes! even before the result! It can't fail!

Denise Friend, NSW

Dear Dianne

I've just finished reading your book Fat Free Forever! *It was great, you did a great job, it's easy to understand and it makes sense…*

I am 39 years old, 163 centimetres tall and started off weighing 85 kilograms. I lost 4 kilograms while on holiday a few weeks ago when I started your program.

Annette Vidic, South Australia

Dear Dianne

I purchased your book Fat Free Forever! *after seeing you on the Bert Newton Show. I have been following the diet and think it's excellent!*

Nella Gerick, Victoria

Dear Dianne

I just wanted to say that I really loved the book you wrote. Thank you very much for it. I have always been obsessed about my weight. I used to always think I was too fat and I started going on diets and not eating at all.

My friends have read your book too and they loved it as well. It's working and I can notice it. Thanks again, and next time I'm in Australia I hope to meet you.

Sonja Dissanayeke, Sri Lanka, aged 16